Semantic Domains in Computational Linguistics

Alfio Gliozzo · Carlo Strapparava

Semantic Domains in Computational Linguistics

Springer

Dr. Alfio Gliozzo
FBK-irst
Via Sommarive 18
38050 Povo-Trento
Italy
gliozzo@fbk.eu

Dr. Carlo Strapparava
FBK-irst
Via Sommarive 18
38050 Povo-Trento
Italy
strappa@fbk.eu

ISBN 978-3-540-68156-4 e-ISBN 978-3-540-68158-8
DOI 10.1007/978-3-540-68158-8
Springer Dordrecht Heidelberg London New York

Library of Congress Control Number: 2009930840

ACM Computing Classification (1998): I.2.7, H.3.1, J.5

Cover design: KuenkelLopka GmbH

Printed on acid-free paper

Springer is part of Springer Science+Business Media (www.springer.com)

Preface

Ambiguity and variability are two basic and pervasive phenomena characterizing lexical semantics. In this book we introduce a computational model for lexical semantics based on Semantic Domains. This concept is inspired by the "Theory of Semantic Fields", proposed in structural linguistics to explain lexical semantics. The main property of Semantic Domains is lexical coherence, i.e. the property of domain-related words to co-occur in texts. This allows us to define automatic acquisition procedures for Domain Models from corpora, and the acquired models provide a shallow representation for lexical ambiguity and variability. Domain Models have been used to define a similarity metric among texts and terms in the Domain Space, where second-order relations are reflected. Topic similarity estimation is at the basis of text comprehension, allowing us to define a very general domain-driven methodology. The basic argument we put forward to support our approach is that the information provided by the Domain Models can be profitably used to boost the performances of supervised Natural Language Processing systems for many tasks. In fact, Semantic Domains allows us to extract domain features for texts, terms and concepts. The obtained indexing, adopted by the Domain Kernel to estimate topic similarity, preserves the original information while reducing the dimensionality of the feature space. The Domain Kernel is used to define a semi-supervised learning algorithm for Text Categorization that achieves state-of-the-art results while decreasing by one order the quantity of labeled texts required for learning. The property of the Domain Space to represent together terms and texts allows us to define an Intensional Learning schema for Text Categorization, in which categories are described by means of discriminative words instead of labeled examples, achieving performances close to human agreement. Then we investigate the role of domain information in Word Sense Disambiguation, developing both unsupervised and supervised approaches that strongly rely on the notion of Semantic Domain. The former is based on the lexical resource WordNet Domains and the latter exploits both sense tagged and unlabeled data to model the relevant domain distinctions among word senses. The proposed supervised approach improves the state-of-the-art performance in many tasks for different languages, while reducing appreciably the amount of sense tagged data required for learning. Finally, we present a lexical acquisition procedure to obtain Multilingual Domain Models from comparable corpora. We exploit such models to approach a Cross-language Text Categorization task, achieving very promising results.

We would first of all acknowledge the effort of other people involved in the eight years' long daily work required to produce the experimental results reported in this monograph, and in particular Claudio Giuliano, who performed most of the experimental work for the WSD experiments, allowing us to achieve very accurate results in competitions due to his patience and skills; to Bernardo Magnini, who first proposed the concept of Semantic Domain, opening the direction we have followed during our research path and supporting it with financial contributions from his projects; and to Ido Dagan, who greatly contributed to the intensional learning framework defining the experimental settings and clarifying the statistical properties of the GM algorithm.

Special thanks are devoted to Oliviero Stock, for his daily encouragement and for the appreciation he has shown for our work; to Walter Daelemans, who demonstrated a real interest in the epistemological aspects of this work from the early stages; to Maurizio Matteuzzi, whose contribution was crucial to interpret the theoretical background of this work related to philosophy of language; to Roberto Basili who immediately understood the potential of Semantic Domains and creatively applied our framework for technology transfer, contributing to highlighting limitations and potentialities; and to Aldo Gangemi, who more recently helped us in clarifying the relationship of this work with formal semantics and knowledge representation.

Last, but not least, we would like to thank our families and parents for having understood with patience our crazy lives, and our friends for having spent their nights in esoteric and sympathetic discussions.

Trento,
September 2008

Alfio Gliozzo
Carlo Strapparava

Contents

1

Introduction

During the ACL 2005 conference, the lifetime achievement award of the Association for Computational Linguistics was assigned to Martin Kay. In his talk, he remarked on the distinction between *Computational Linguistics* and *Natural Language Processing* (NLP). Computational Linguistics is about using computers to investigate linguistic theory, while the NLP field concerns the engineering of text processing applications to solve particular tasks for practical reasons. Computational Linguistics is then a science, while NLP is the set of all its technological implications. Computational Linguistics is a branch of general linguistics, while NLP is more properly an engineering problem.

During recent decades, there was some confusion, mostly because of the increasing popularity of empirical methods for text processing. In fact, the expectation of a large portion of the community was that the supervised approach would be successfully applied to any linguistic problem, as long as enough training material was made available. This belief was motivated by the excellent performance achieved by supervised approaches to many traditional NLP tasks, such as Part of Speech Tagging, Machine Translation, Text Categorization, Parsing and many others. Research on empirical methods for NLP has been encouraged by the increasing need for text processing technologies in the Web era. This has induced the community to find some cheap and fast solutions to practical problems, such as mail categorization, question answering and speech recognition. As a result, limited effort has been invested in understanding the basic underlying linguistic phenomena, and the problem of studying the language by exploiting computational approaches (i.e. Computational Linguistics) has been confused with that of implementing useful text processing technologies.

The "crisis" of empirical methods in linguistics is a matter of recent debate. Most of the research directions that were started in the 1990s have now been fully explored, and further improvements are becoming harder and harder because of the low generality of the proposed models. Such models, in general, do not capture the essential "nature" of the phenomena involved, and most of the effort has been spent in improving the machine learning devices

A. Gliozzo and C. Strapparava, *Semantic Domains in Computational Linguistics*,
DOI: 10.1007/978-3-540-68158-8_1, © Springer-Verlag Berlin Heidelberg 2009

and in feature engineering stuff. The main drawback of this lack of theory is the huge amount of training data required for learning, which makes infeasible the application of supervised technology to practical settings because of the high development costs of the annotated resources. In addition, the novel text processing systems required for the Semantic Web are expected to perform a deeper semantic analysis, for example by inducing domain-specific ontologies from texts and exploiting inferential processes, which can hardly be modeled by simply following a strictly empirical approach. We believe that any empirical approach to computational semantics is destined to fail if it is not supported by a clear understanding of the relevant underlying linguistic phenomena involved in the task to which it is applied.

On the other hand, empirical approaches have significantly enriched Computational Linguistics from a methodological point of view. The empirical framework provides us with a set of ideal benchmarks where linguistic theories can be corroborated, accepted or rejected in a systematic and objective way. In addition, the task oriented evaluation fits perfectly with the *meaning-is-use* assumption, claiming that the meaning of expressions is fully determined by their use. Accepting this assumption prevents us from performing a "static" evaluation, based on subjective judgments of speakers, because meaning is first of all a behavior, situated in a concrete form of life. In our opinion, the only way to evaluate linguistic theories in computational semantics is through a task-based application of their models. In addition, the great amount of empirical studies produced in the recent NLP literature is a very useful source of observations and empirical laws, which can be analyzed and explained to propose more general linguistic theories.

It is our opinion that Computational Linguistics should return to its origins of scientific investigation about language phenomena without forgetting the lesson learned from empirical approaches. Its main goal is to corroborate linguistic models and theories, designing algorithms and systems that can be extensively evaluated on well defined and objective NLP tasks. Of course, the better the proposed model, the more general its range of applications. A good linguistic theory should be able to explain many phenomena; a good computational model should be exploited uniformly across different tasks.

The present work is about Semantic Domains, a computational model for lexical semantics, and shows a paradigmatic example of the methodological claims already depicted. Semantic Domains are inspired by the "Theory of Semantic Fields", proposed in structural linguistics in the 1930s. Semantic Domains can be used to induce lexical representations from corpora that can be easily exploited in many NLP tasks. Throughout this book we will shift from a theoretical point of view to a more technological perspective, with the double aim of evaluating our linguistic claims and developing state-of-the-art technologies. The main evidence supporting Semantic Domains in lexical semantics is the possibility of exploiting them uniformly across different NLP tasks. The reciprocal interactions between engineering and theory allow us to corroborate the proposed model, while inducing new phenomena and research directions.

1.1 Lexical Semantics and Text Understanding

Ambiguity and variability are two of the most basic and pervasive phenomena characterizing lexical semantics. A word is ambiguous when its meaning varies depending on the context in which it occurs. Variability is the fact that the same concept can be referred to by different terms. Most of the words in texts are ambiguous, and most of the concepts can be expressed by different terms. The pervasiveness of such phenomena leads us to design NLP systems dealing with them.

In the NLP literature, the problem to assign concepts to words in texts has been called Word Sense Disambiguation (WSD). WSD is a crucial task in Computational Linguistics, and has been investigated for years by the community without leading to a definitive conclusion. Any automatic WSD methodology has to deal with at least the following two problems: (i) defining an adequate sense repository to describe the concepts involved in the application domain and (ii) designing a well-performing WSD algorithm to assign the correct concepts to words in contexts. Both problems are very hard to solve and very strongly related.

Ambiguity and variability can be represented by defining a two-layer lexical description that puts into relation words and concepts. Ambiguous words are associated to more than one concept, and synonyms are related to the same concept. The structure so obtained is a semantic network that can be used for computational purposes, as for example WordNet [66]. In the WordNet model, lexical concepts (i.e. concepts denoted by one or more terms in the language) are represented by means of synsets (i.e. sets of synonyms) and they are related to each other by means of paradigmatic relations, as for example hyponymy and meronomy.

The WordNet model was conceived in the more general framework of structural semantics, claiming that meaning emerges from word oppositions. As far as computational semantic is concerned, the structural approach is the most viable framework, because it allows us to define lexical meaning by means of internal relations only, avoiding any "external" reference to world knowledge that cannot be represented by means of the language itself.

To find an adequate representation for lexical semantics is not easy, especially as far as open domain applications are concerned. In fact, exhaustive lexical resources, such as WordNet, are always characterized by subjectivity and incompleteness: irrelevant senses and gaps with respect to the application domain are very difficult to avoid. The quality of the lexical representation affects drastically the WSD performances. In fact, if the lexical resource contains too fine grained sense distinctions, the inter-tagger agreement on the task will be very low. In addition, many central concepts for the application domain are often not covered by the lexical resource.

If words in texts were automatically connected to the concepts of external ontologies, a very large amount of additional knowledge would be accessed by NLP systems. For example, a bilingual dictionary is a very useful knowledge source for Machine Translation, and systems for information access could use dictionaries for query expansion and Cross-language Retrieval. Modeling variability helps topics be detected for Text Categorization, allowing the system to recognize similarities among texts even if they do not share any word. Lexical semantic is then at the basis of text understanding. Words in texts are just the "tip of the iceberg" of a wider semantic structure representing the language. Any computational model for text comprehension should take into account not only the concepts explicitly expressed in texts, but also all those concepts connected to them, highlighting the relevant portion of the underlying lexical structure describing the application domain.

We believe that any serious attempt to solve the WSD problem has to start by providing a theoretically motivated model for ambiguity and variability. The main goal of this book is to get some computational insights into this.

1.2 Semantic Domains: Computational Models for Lexical Semantics

The main limitation of the structural approach in lexical semantics is that any word is potentially related to any other word in the lexicon. The lexicon is conceived as a whole, word meaning comes out from their relations with other terms in the language. The huge number of relations so generated is a relevant problem both from a lexicographic and from a computational point of view. In fact, the task of analyzing the relations among all the words in the lexicon is very hard, because of the high number of word pairs that should be compared.

The "Theory of Semantic Fields" [87] is a step toward the definition of a model for lexical semantics. It was proposed by Jost Trier in the 1930s in the structural view, and it is well-known in the linguistic literature. In synthesis, this theory claims that words are structured into a set of Semantic Fields. Semantic Fields define the extent to which paradigmatic relations hold, partitioning the lexicon among regions of highly associated concepts, while words belonging to different fields are basically unrelated.

This theory is becoming a matter of recent interest in Computational Linguistics [56, 59, 32], because it opens new directions to represent and to acquire lexical information. In this book we propose a computational framework for lexical semantics that strongly relies on this theory. We start our investigation with observing that Semantic Fields are lexically-coherent, i.e. the words they contain tend to co-occur in texts. The lexical coherence assumption has led us to define the concept of Semantic Domain, the main topic of this book.

Semantic Domains are fields characterized by lexically coherent words. The lexical coherence assumption can be exploited for computational purposes, because it allows us to define automatic acquisition procedures from corpora. Once the lexical constituents of a given domain have been identified, a further structure among them, i.e. a domain-specific ontology, can be defined by simply looking for "internal" relations, according to the diktat of the semantic field theory. We do not approach the full problem of ontology learning, restricting our attention to the subtask of identifying the membership relations among words in the lexicon and a set of Semantic Domains.

To this aim we propose a very simple data structure, namely the Domain Model (DM), consisting of a matrix describing the degree of association between terms and semantic domains. Once a DM is available, for example by acquiring it from unsupervised learning or by exploiting manually annotated lexical resources, it can be profitably used to approach many NLP tasks. The basic argument we put forward to support our domain-based approach is that the information provided by the DMs can be profitably used to boost the performances of NLP systems for many tasks, such as Text Categorization, Word Sense Disambiguation and Cross-language Text Categorization. In fact, DMs allow us to define a more informed topic similarity metric among texts, by representing them by means of vectors in a Domain Space, in which second order relations among terms are reflected. Topic similarity estimation is at the basis of text comprehension, allowing us to define a very general domain-driven methodology that can be exploited uniformly among different tasks.

Another very relevant property of Semantic Domains is their interlinguality. It allows us to define Multilingual Domain Models, representing domain relations among words in different languages. It is possible to acquire such models from comparable corpora, without exploiting manually annotated resources or bilingual dictionaries. Multilingual Domain Models have been successfully applied to approach a Cross-language Text Categorization task.

1.3 Structure of the Book

The present book is about Semantic Domains in Computational Linguistics. Its main goal is to provide a general overview of long-standing research we have worked on at ITC-irst, originating from the annotation of the lexical resource WordNet Domains and then followed up by the most recent corpus-based direction of empirical learning. The research we are going to present is quite complex because it pertains to many different aspects of the problem. In fact, on one hand it is basically a Computational Linguistics work, because it presents a computational model for lexical semantics based on Semantic Domains and it investigates their basic properties; on the other hand it is an NLP study, because it proposes new technologies to develop state-of-the-art systems for many different NLP tasks. As remarked at the beginning of this section, the task-based evaluation is the basic argument to support our claims, which we try to summarize below:

1. Semantic Domains are Semantic Fields characterized by high lexical coherence. The concepts denoted by words in the same field are strongly connected among each other, while words belonging to different fields denote basically unrelated concepts.
2. DMs represent lexical ambiguity and variability. In fact if a word occurs in texts belonging to different domains it refers to different concepts (ambiguity), while two terms can be substituted (variability) only if they belong to the same domain.
3. Semantic Domains can be acquired from corpora in a totally unsupervised way by analyzing the co-occurrences of words in documents.
4. Semantic Domains allow us to extract domain features for texts, terms and concepts. The obtained index improves topic similarity estimation because it preserves the original information while reducing the dimensionality of the learning space. As an effect, the amount of labeled data required for learning is minimized.
5. WSD systems benefit from a domain-based feature representation. In fact, as claimed by point 2, sense distinctions are partially motivated by domain variations.
6. Semantic Domains are basically multilingual, and can be used to relate terms in different languages. Domain relations among terms in different languages can be used for Cross-language Text Categorization, while they are not expressive enough to represent deeper multilingual information, such as translation pairs.

In the rest of this section we summarize the main points of this book, highlighting their contributions to support the claims we have pointed out above.

1.3.1 Semantic Domains

We start our inquiry by presenting the "Theory of Semantic Fields" [88], a structural model for lexical semantics proposed in the first half of the twentieth century. Semantic Fields constitute the linguistic background of this work, and will be discussed in detail in Sect. 2.1, where we illustrate their properties and we offer a literature review.

Then we introduce the concept of *Semantic Domain* [59] as an extension of the concept of Semantic Field from a lexical level, in which it identifies a set of domain-related lexical concepts, to a textual level, in which it identifies a class of similar documents. The founding idea of Semantic Domains is the lexical coherence property that guarantees the existence of Semantic Domains in corpora. The basic hypothesis of lexical coherence is that a large portion of the lexical concepts in the same text belongs to the same domain. This intuition is largely supported by the results of our experiments performed on a sense-tagged corpus (i.e. SemCor) showing that concepts in texts tend to belong to a small number of relevant domains. In addition we demonstrate a "one domain per discourse" hypothesis, claiming that multiple uses of a word in a coherent portion of text tend to share the same domain.

In Sect. 2.4, we focus on the problem of defining a set of requirements that should be satisfied by any "ideal" domain set: *completeness*, *balancement* and *separability*. Such a requirement follows from the textual interpretation allowed by the lexical coherence assumption. An example of domain annotation is WordNet Domains, an extension of WordNet [25], in which each synset in WordNet is marked with one or more domain labels, belonging to a predefined domain set. WordNet Domains is just one of the possible computational models we can define to represent Semantic Domains. Such models are asked to describe the domain relations in at least one of the following (symmetric) levels: text level, concept level and term level. Correspondingly the following models have been proposed in the literature: text annotation, concept annotation, topic signatures and Domain Vectors. Section 2.7 is entirely devoted to illustrate such issues.

1.3.2 Domain Models

One of the possibilities to represent domain information at the lexical level is to define Domain Models (DMs). They describe the domain relations at the term level and can be exploited to estimate topic similarity among texts and terms. A DM is a matrix in which rows are indexed by words and columns are associated with Semantic Domains. The cells in the matrix represent the domain relevance of words with respect to the corresponding domains. DMs are shallow models for lexical semantics, because they capture partially the phenomena of variability and ambiguity. In fact, domain ambiguity is just one of the aspects of the more general phenomenon of lexical ambiguity, and domain relations allow us to identify classes of domain-related words recalling similar concepts, even if they do not refer to exactly the same concept.

Once a DM has been determined, it is possible to define a Domain Space, a geometrical space in which both texts and terms can be represented by means of vectors and then compared. The Domain Space improves the classical text representation adopted in Information Retrieval, where texts are represented in a vectorial space indexed by words, i.e. the Vector Space Model (VSM). In particular, domain information allows us to deal with variability and ambiguity, avoiding sparseness.

A DM is fully specified whenever a domain set is selected, and a domain relevance function among terms and domains is provided. To this aim we followed two alternative directions: adopting available lexical resources and inducing them from corpora.

The lexical resource WordNet Domains, described in Sect. 2.5, contains all the information required to infer a DM, as illustrated in Sect. 3.4. The WordNet-based DM presents several drawbacks, both from a theoretical and from an applicative point of view: the DM is fixed, the domain set of WordNet Domains is far from complete, balanced and separated; and the lexicon represented by the DM is limited to the terms in WordNet.

To overcome these limitations we propose the use of corpus-based acquisition techniques, such as Term Clustering. In principle, any Term Clustering algorithm can be adopted to acquire a DM from a large corpus. Our solution is to exploit Latent Semantic Analysis (LSA), because it allows us to perform this operation in a very efficient way, capturing lexical coherence. LSA is a very well known technique that was originally developed to estimate the similarity among texts and terms in a corpus. In Sect. 3.6 we exploit its basic assumptions to define the Term Clustering algorithm we used to acquire the DMs required to perform our experiments.

DMs can be exploited inside a supervised learning framework, in order to provide "external" knowledge to supervised systems for NLP, which can be profitably used for topic similarity estimation. We will define a Domain Kernel, a similarity function among terms and texts that can be exploited by any kernel-based learning algorithm, with the effect of avoiding the problems of lexical variability and ambiguity, minimizing the quantity of training data required for learning.

1.3.3 Semantic Domains in Text Categorization

Many NLP tasks can be modeled as classification problems, consisting of assigning category labels to linguistic objects. For example, the Text Categorization task [80] is about classifying documents according to a set of semantic classes, domains in our terminology.

The Domain Kernel performs an explicit dimensionality reduction of the input space, by mapping the vectors from the VSM into the Domain Space, improving the generalization capability of the learning algorithm and then reducing the amount of training data required for training. The main advantage of adopting domain features is that they allow a dimensionality reduction while preserving, and sometimes increasing, the information provided by the "classical" VSM representation. This property is crucial from a machine learning perspective because it allows us to reduce the amount of training data required for learning.

Adopting the Domain Kernel in a supervised learning framework is a way to perform semi-supervised learning, because both unlabeled and labeled data are exploited for learning. In fact, we acquire DMs from unlabeled data, and then we exploit them to estimate the similarity among labeled examples.

Text Categorization experiments show that DMs, acquired from unlabeled data, allow us to uniformly improve the similarity estimation among documents, with the basic effect of increasing the recall while preserving the precision of the algorithm. This effect is particularly evident when just small amounts of labeled data are provided for learning. A comparison with the state-of-the-art shows that the Domain Kernel achieves better or similar performances, while it reduces the amount of training data required for learning.

Finally we concentrate on the more difficult problem of categorizing texts without exploiting labeled training data. In this setting, categories are described by providing sets of relevant terms, termed *intensional descriptions*, and a training corpus of unlabeled texts is provided for learning. We have called this learning schema *Intensional Learning* (IL). The definition of the Domain Kernel fits perfectly the IL settings. In fact, unlabeled texts can be used to acquire DMs, and the Domain Kernel can be exploited to compare the similarity among the terms in the intensional descriptions and the unlabeled texts, performing a preliminary categorization of the unlabeled data. The duality property of the Domain Space allows us to compare directly terms and texts, in order to select a preliminary set of documents for each category, from which to start a bootstrap process. We applied and evaluated our algorithm on some Text Categorization tasks, obtaining competitive performance using only the category names as initial seeds. Interesting results were revealed when comparing our IL method to a state-of-the-art supervised classifier, trained on manually labeled documents. It required 70 (Reuters data set) or 160 (Newsgroup data set) documents per category to achieve the same performance that IL obtained by using only the category names. These results suggest that IL may provide an appealing cost-effective alternative when sub-optimal accuracy suffices, or when it is too costly or impractical to obtain sufficient labeled training data.

1.3.4 Semantic Domains in Word Sense Disambiguation

Semantic Domains provide an effective solution for the Knowledge Acquisition Bottleneck problem affecting supervised WSD systems. Semantic Domains are a general linguistic notion that can be modeled independently from the specific words, and then applied uniformly to model sense distinctions for any word in the lexicon. A major portion of the information required for sense disambiguation corresponds to domain relations among words. Many of the features that contribute to disambiguation identify the domains that characterize a particular sense or subset of senses. For example, economics terms provide characteristic features for the financial senses of words like *bank* and *interest*, while legal terms characterize the judicial sense of *sentence* and *court*.

In addition, Semantic Domains provide a useful coarse-grained level of sense distinction, to be profitably used in a wide range of applications that do not require the finer grained distinctions typically reported in dictionaries. In fact, senses of the same words that belong to the same domain, as for example the `institution` and the `building` sense of `bank`, are very closely related. In many NLP tasks, as for example Information Retrieval, it is not necessary to distinguish among them. Grouping together senses having similar domains is then a way to define a coarse-grained sense distinction, that can be disambiguated more easily.

In practical application scenarios it is infeasible to collect enough training material for WSD, due to the very high annotation cost of sense tagged corpora. Improving the WSD performance with little learning is then a fundamental issue to be solved to design supervised WSD systems for real world problems. To achieve this goal, we identified two promising research directions:

1. Modeling independently domain and syntagmatic aspects of sense distinction.
2. Leveraging external knowledge acquired from unlabeled corpora [29].

The first direction is motivated by the linguistic assumption that syntagmatic and domain (associative) relations are both crucial to represent sense distinctions, while they are basically originated by very different phenomena. Regarding the second direction, external knowledge would be required to help WSD algorithms in generalizing over the data available for training. In particular, domain knowledge can be modeled independently from the particular word expert classifier by performing term clustering operations, and then exploited for WSD to produce a generalized feature space, reflecting the domain aspects of sense distinction.

We will present and evaluate both unsupervised and supervised WSD approaches that strongly depend on the notion of Semantic Domain. The former is based on the lexical resource WORDNET DOMAINS and the latter exploits both sense tagged and unlabeled data to model the relevant domain distinctions among word senses. At the moment, both techniques achieve the state-of-the-art in WSD.

Our unsupervised WSD approach is called Domain-Driven Disambiguation (DDD), a generic WSD methodology that utilizes only domain information to perform WSD. For this reason DDD is not able to capture sense distinctions that depend on syntagmatic relations, while it represents a viable solution to perform a domain grained WSD that can be profitably used by a wide range of applications, such as Information Retrieval and User Modeling [57]. DDD can be performed in a totally unsupervised way once Semantic Domains have been associated to each sense of the word to be disambiguated. The DDD methodology is very simple, and consists of selecting the word sense whose domain maximizes the similarity with the domain of the context in which the word occurs. The operation of determining the domain of a text is called Domain Relevance Estimation, and is performed by adopting the IL algorithm for Text Categorization presented in Sect. 4.2. Experiments show that disambiguation at the domain level is substantially more accurate, while the accuracy of DDD for the fine-grained sense distinctions may not be good enough for various applications. Disambiguation at domain granularity is sufficiently practical using only domain information with the unsupervised DDD method alone, even with no training examples.

We will present a semi-supervised approach to WSD that exploits DMs, acquired from unlabeled data, to approach lexical sample tasks. It is developed in the framework of Kernel Methods by defining a kernel combination, in order to take into account different aspects of sense distinction simultaneously and independently. In particular we combined a set of syntagmatic kernels, estimating the similarity among word sequences in the local context of the word to be disambiguated, to a Domain Kernel, measuring the similarity among the topics of the wider contexts in which the word occurs. The Domain Kernel exploits DMs acquired from untagged occurrences of the word to be disambiguated. Its impact on the overall performances of the kernel combination is crucial, allowing our system to achieve the state-of-the-art in the field. As for the Text Categorization experiments, the learning curve improves sensibly when DMs are used, opening new research perspectives to implement minimally supervised WSD systems, to be applied to all-words tasks, where fewer amounts of training data are in general available.

1.3.5 Multilingual Domain Models

The last topic is about the multilingual aspects of Semantic Domains. Multilinguality was claimed for Semantic Fields by Trier himself, and has been presupposed in the development of WordNet Domains, where domain information has been assigned to the concepts of the multilingual index in MultiWordNet.

Our basic hypothesis is that comparable corpora in different languages are characterized by the same domain set. It reflects at the lexical level, allowing us to define Multilingual Domain Models (MDMs). MDMs are represented by means of matrices, describing the associations among terms in different languages and a domain set.

MDMs can be acquired in several ways, depending on the available lexical resources and corpora. For example they can be derived from the information in WordNet Domains, from parallel corpora and from comparable corpora. We concentrate on the latter approach, because we believe it is more attractive from an application point of view: it is easier to collect comparable corpora than parallel corpora, because no manual intervention is required. To perform this operation we hypothesize that most of the proper nouns, relevant entities and words that have not been lexicalized yet, are expressed by using the same terms in different languages, preserving the original spelling. As a consequence, the same entities will be denoted with the same words in different languages, allowing us to automatically detect couples of translation pairs just by looking at the word shape [48]. The words in common to the vocabularies of the different languages can be exploited to obtain a set of translation pairs that can be used as "seeds" to start a generalization process to infer domain relations among words in different languages.

We claim that the information provided by such word pairs is enough to detect domain relations, while deeper relations cannot be captured so easily.

To demonstrate this claim we evaluated the quality of the acquired MDMs on a Cross-language Text Categorization task, consisting of training a Text Categorization system using labeled examples in a source language (e.g. *English*), and of classifying documents in a different target language (e.g. *Italian*) adopting a common category set. MDMs were acquired from the whole training set by exploiting an unsupervised methodology, and a Multilingual Domain Kernel, defined by analogy with the Domain Kernel adopted in the monolingual settings, was compared to a bag-of-words approach that we regarded as a baseline. The results were surprisingly good, allowing the Multilingual Domain Kernel to largely surpass the baseline approach, demonstrating the benefits of our acquisition methodology and, indirectly, the multilingual hypothesis we formulated about Semantic Domains.

1.3.6 Kernel Methods for Natural Language Processing

Most of the systems we implemented to evaluate our claims were developed in the supervised learning framework of Kernel Methods. Kernel Methods are a class of learning algorithms that depend on the definition of kernel functions. Kernel functions compute the similarities among the objects in the instance space, and constitute a viable alternative to feature-based approaches that model the problem by defining explicit feature extraction techniques. We are going to present an introduction to kernel-based supervised classifiers, and to describe a set of basic kernel functions that can be used for NLP. Our approach is to model linguistic fundamentals independently, and then combine them by exploiting a kernel combination schema to develop the final application.

2

Semantic Domains

In this chapter we define the concept of Semantic Domain, recently introduced in Computational Linguistics [56] and successfully exploited in NLP [29]. This notion is inspired by the "Theory of Semantic Fields" [88], a structural model for lexical semantics proposed by Jost Trier at the beginning of the last century. The basic assumption is that the lexicon is structured into Semantic Fields: semantic relations among concepts belonging to the same field are very dense, while concepts belonging to different fields are typically unrelated. The theory of Semantic Fields constitutes the linguistic background of this work, and will be discussed in detail in Sect. 2.1. The main limitation of this theory is that it does not provide an objective criterion to distinguish among Semantic Fields. The concept of linguistic game allows us to formulate such a criterion, by observing that linguistic games are reflected by texts in corpora.

Even if Semantic Fields have been deeply investigated in structural linguistics, computational approaches for them have been proposed quite recently by introducing the concept of *Semantic Domain* [59]. Semantic Domains are clusters of terms and texts that exhibit a high level of lexical coherence, i.e. the property of domain-specific words to co-occur together in texts. In the present work, we will refer to these kinds of relations among terms, concepts and texts by means of the term *Domain Relations*, adopting the terminology introduced by [56].

The concept of Semantic Domain extends the concept of Semantic Field from a lexical level, in which it identifies a set of domain related lexical concepts, to a textual level, in which it identifies a class of similar documents. The founding idea is the lexical coherence assumption, that has to be presupposed to guarantee the existence of Semantic Domains in corpora.

This chapter is structured as follows. First of all we discuss the notion of Semantic Field from a linguistic point of view, reporting the basics of Trier's work and some alternative views proposed by structural linguists, then we illustrate some interesting connections with the concept of linguistic game (see Sect. 2.2), that justify our further corpus-based approach. In Sect. 2.3

A. Gliozzo and C. Strapparava, *Semantic Domains in Computational Linguistics*,
DOI: 10.1007/978-3-540-68158-8_2, © Springer-Verlag Berlin Heidelberg 2009

we introduce the notion of Semantic Domain. Then, in Sect. 2.4, we focus on the problem of defining a set of requirements that should be satisfied by any "ideal" domain set: *completeness*, *balancement* and *separability*. In Sect. 2.5 we present the lexical resource WordNet Domains, a large scale repository of domain information for lexical concepts. In Sect. 2.6 we analyze the relations between Semantic Domains at the lexical and at the textual levels, describing the property of *Lexical Coherence* in texts. We will provide empirical evidence for it, by showing that most of the lexicon in documents belongs to the principal domain of the text, giving support to the *One Domain per Discourse* hypothesis. The lexical coherence assumption holds for a wide class of words, namely *domain words*, whose senses can be mainly disambiguated by considering the domain in which they are located, regardless of any further syntactic information. Finally, we report a literature review describing all the computational approaches to represent and exploit Semantic Domains we have found in the literature.

2.1 The Theory of Semantic Fields

Semantic Domains are a matter of recent interest in Computational Linguistics [56, 59, 29], even though their basic assumptions are inspired from a long standing research direction in structural linguistics started in the beginning of the last century and widely known as "The Theory of Semantic Fields" [55]. The notion of *Semantic Field* has proved its worth in a great volume of studies, and has been mainly put forward by Jost Trier [87], whose work is credited with having "opened a new phase in the history of semantics" [89].

In that work, it has been claimed that the lexicon is structured in clusters of very closely related concepts, lexicalized by sets of words. Word senses are determined and delimitated only by the meanings of other words in the same field. Such clusters of semantically related terms have been called Semantic Fields,[1] and the theory explaining their properties is known as "The theory of Semantic Fields" [92].

This theory has been developed in the general framework of Saussure's structural semantics [20], whose basic claim is that a word meaning is determined by the "horizontal" paradigmatic and the "vertical" syntagmatic relations between that word and others in the whole language [55]. Structural semantics is the predominant epistemological paradigm in linguistics, and it is very much appreciated in Computational Linguistic. For example, many machine readable dictionaries describe the word senses by means of semantic networks representing relations among terms (e.g. WordNet [66]). The Semantic Fields Theory goes a step further in the structural approach to lexical

[1] There is no agreement on the terminology adopted by different authors. Trier uses the German term *wortfeld* (literally "word field" or "lexical field" in Lyons' terminology) to denote what we call here semantic field.

semantics by introducing an additional aggregation level and by delimiting to what extent paradigmatic relations hold.

Semantic Fields are conceptual regions shared out amongst a number of words. Each field is viewed as a partial region of the whole expanse of ideas that is covered by the vocabulary of a language. Such areas are referred to by groups of semantically related words, i.e. the Semantic Fields. Internally to each field, a word meaning is determined by the network of relations established with other words.

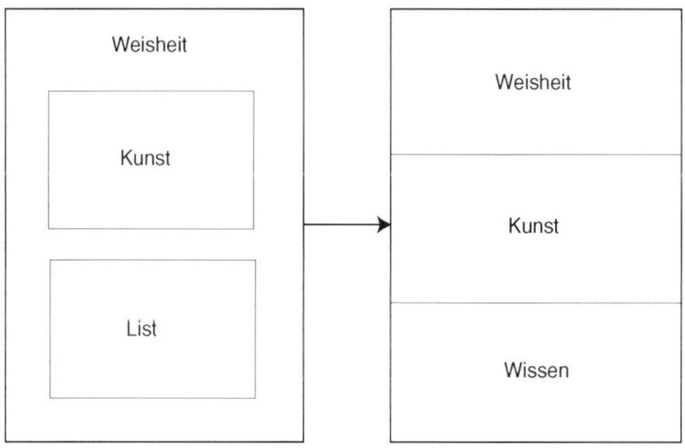

Fig. 2.1. The INTELLECTUAL field's structure in German at around 1200 AD (left) and at around 1300 AD (right)

Trier provided an example of its theory by studying the INTELLECTUAL field in German, illustrated in Fig. 2.1. Around 1200, the words composing the field were organized around three key terms: Weisheit, Kunst and List. Kunst meant knowledge of courtly and chivalric attainments, whereas List meant knowledge outside that sphere. Weisheit was their hypernym, including the meaning of both. One hundred years later a different picture emerged. The courtly world has disintegrated, so there was no longer a need for a distinction between courtly and non-courtly skills. List has moved towards its modern meaning (i.e. `cunning`) and has lost its intellectual connotations; then it is not yet included into the INTELLECTUAL field. Kunst has also moved towards its modern meaning indicating the result of artistic attainments. The term Weisheit now denotes religious or mystical experiences, and Wissen is a more general term denoting `knowledge`. This example clearly shows that word meaning is determined only by internal relations between the lexicon of the field, and that the conceptual area to which each word refers is delimitated in opposition with the meaning of other concepts in the lexicon.

A relevant limitation of Trier's work is that a clear distinction between lexical and conceptual fields is not explicitly done. The lexical field is the set of words belonging to the semantic field, while the conceptual field is the set of concepts covered by terms of the field. Lexical fields and conceptual fields are radically different, because they are composed by different objects. From an analysis of their reciprocal connections, many interesting aspects of lexical semantics emerge, as for example ambiguity and variability. The different senses of ambiguous words should be necessarily located into different conceptual fields, because they are characterized by different relations with different words. It reflects the fact that ambiguous words are located into more than one lexical field. On the other hand, variability can be modeled by observing that synonymous terms refer to the same concepts, then they will be necessarily located in the same lexical field. The terms contained in the same lexical field recall each other. Thus, the distribution of words among different lexical fields is a relevant aspect to be taken into account to identify word senses. Understanding words in contexts is mainly the operation of locating them in the appropriate conceptual fields.

Regarding the connection between lexical and conceptual fields, we observe that most of the words characterizing a Semantic Field are domain-specific terms, then they are not ambiguous. Monosemic words are located only into one field, and correspond univocally to the denoted concepts. As an approximation, conceptual fields can be analyzed by studying the corresponding lexical fields. The correspondence between conceptual and lexical fields is of great interest for computational approaches to lexical semantics. In fact, the basic objects manipulated by most text processing systems are words. The connection between conceptual and lexical fields can then be exploited to shift from a lexical representation to a deeper conceptual analysis.

Trier also hypothesized that Semantic Fields are related between each other, so as to compose a higher level structure, that together with the low level structures internal to each field composes the structure of the whole lexicon. The structural relations among Semantic Fields are much more stable than the low level relations established among words. For example, the meaning of the words in the INTELLECTUAL field has changed largely in a limited period of time, but the INTELLECTUAL field itself has pretty much preserved the same conceptual area. This observation explains the fact that Semantic Fields are often consistent among languages, cultures and time.

As a consequence there exists a strong correspondence among Semantic Fields of different languages, while such a strong correspondence cannot be established among the terms themselves. For example, the lexical field of COLORS is structured differently in different languages, and sometimes it is very difficult, if not impossible, to translate names of colors, even whether the chromatic spectrum perceived by people in different countries (i.e. the conceptual field) is the same. Some languages adopt many words to denote the chromatic range to which the English term `white` refers, distinguishing among different degrees of "whiteness" that have no direct translation in English. Anyway, the chromatic range covered by the COLORS fields of different languages is evidently the same. The meaning of each term is defined by virtue of its opposition with other terms of the same field. Different languages have different distinctions, but the field of COLORS itself is a constant among all the languages.

Another implication of the Semantic Fields Theory is that words belonging to different fields are basically unrelated. In fact, a word meaning is established only by the network of relations among the terms of its field. As far as paradigmatic relations are concerned, two words belonging to different fields are then unrelated. This observation is crucial form a methodological point of view. The practical advantage of adopting the Semantic Field Theory in linguistics is that it allows a large scale structural analysis of the whole lexicon of a language, which is otherwise infeasible. In fact, restricting the attention to a particular lexical field is a way to reduce the complexity of the overall task of finding relations among words in the whole lexicon, that is evidently quadratic in the number of words. The complexity of reiterating this operation for each Semantic Field is much lower than that of analyzing the lexicon as a whole. From a computational point of view, the memory allocation and the computation time required to represent an "all against each other" relation schema is quadratic on the number of words in the language (i.e. $O(|\mathcal{V}|^2)$. The number of operations required to compare only those words belonging to a single field is evidently much lower (i.e. $\mathrm{O}\Big(\big(\frac{|\mathcal{V}|}{d}\big)^2\Big)$, assuming that the vocabulary of the language is partitioned into d Semantic Fields of equal sizes). To cover the whole lexicon, this operation has to be iterated d times. The complexity of the task to analyze the structure of the whole lexicon is then $O\Big(d\big(\frac{|\mathcal{V}|}{d}\big)^2\Big) = O\Big(\frac{|\mathcal{V}|^2}{d}\Big)$. Introducing the additional constraint that the number of words in each field is bounded, where k is the maximum size, we obtain $d \geqslant \frac{|\mathcal{V}|}{k}$. It follows that $O\Big(\frac{|\mathcal{V}|^2}{d}\Big) \leqslant O(|\mathcal{V}|k)$. Assuming that k is an "a priori" constant, determined by the inherent optimization properties required by the domain-specific lexical systems to be coherent, the complexity of the task to analyze the structure of the whole lexicon decreases by one order (i.e. $O(|\mathcal{V}|)$), suggesting an effective methodology to acquire semantic relations among domain-specific concepts from texts

The main limitation of Trier's theory is that it does not provide any objective criterion to identify and delimitate Semantic Fields in the language. The author himself admits "what symptoms, what characteristic features entitle the linguist to assume that in some place or other of the whole vocabulary there is a field? What are the linguistic considerations that guide the grasp with which he selects certain elements as belonging to a field, in order then to examine them as a field?" [88]. The answer to this question is an issue opened by Trier's work, and it has been approached by many authors in the literature.

Trier's theory has been frequently associated to Weisgerber's "theory of contents" [93], claiming that word senses are supposed to be immediately given by virtue of the extra-lingual contexts in which they occur. The main problem of this referential approach is that it is not clear how extra-lingual contexts are provided; then those processes are inexplicable and mysterious.

The referential solution, adopted to explain the field of colors, is straightforward as long as we confine ourselves to fields that are definable with reference to some obvious collection of external objects, but it is not applicable to abstract concepts. The solution proposed by Porzig was to adopt syntagmatic relations to identify word fields [74]. In his view, a Semantic Field is the range of words that are capable of meaningful connection with a given word. In other words, terms belonging to the same field are syntagmatically related to one or more common terms, as for example the set of all the possible subjects or objects for a certain verb, or the set of nouns to which an adjective can be applied. Words in the same field would be distinguished by the difference of their syntagmatic relations with other words.

A less interesting solution has been proposed by Coseriu [15], founded upon the assumption that there is a fundamental analogy between the phonological opposition of sounds and the "lexematic" opposition of meanings. We do not consider this position.

2.2 Semantic Fields and the *meaning-is-use* View

In the previous section we have pointed out that the main limitation of Trier's theory is the gap of an objective criterion to characterize Semantic Fields. The solutions we have found in the literature rely on very obscure notions, of scarce interest from a computational point of view. To overcome such a limitation, in this section we introduce the notion of Semantic Domain (see Sect. 2.3).

The notion of Semantic Domain improves that of Semantic Fields by connecting the structuralist approach in semantics to the *meaning-is-use* assumption introduced by Ludwig Wittgenstein in his celebrated Philosophical Investigations [94]. A word meaning is its use into the concrete "form of life" where it is adopted, i.e. the *linguistic game*, in Wittgenstein's terminology. Words are then meaningful only if they are expressed in concrete and situated linguistic games that provide the conditions for determining the meaning of natural language expressions. To illustrate this concept, Wittgenstein provided a clarifying example describing a very basic linguistic game: "...Let us imagine a language ...The language is meant to serve for communication between a builder A and an assistant B. A is building with building-stones; there are blocks, pillars, slabs and beams. B has to pass the stones, and that in the order in which A needs them. For this purpose they use a language consisting of the words block, pillar, slab, beam. A calls them out; – B brings the stone which he has learnt to bring at such-and-such a call. – Conceive of this as a complete primitive language." [94].

We observe that the notions of linguistic game and Semantic Field show many interesting connections. They approach the same problem from two different points of view, getting to a similar conclusion. According to Trier's view, words are meaningful when they belong to a specific Semantic Field, and their meaning is determined by the structure of the lexicon in the field. According to Wittgenstein's view, words are meaningful when there exists a linguistic game in which they can be formulated, and their meaning is exactly their use. In both cases, meaning arises from the wider contexts in which words are located.

Words appearing frequently in the same linguistic game are likely to be located in the same lexical field. In the previous example the words block, pillar, slab and beam have been used in a common linguistic game, while they clearly belong to the Semantic Field of BUILDING INDUSTRY. This example suggests that the notion of linguistic game provides a criterion to identify and to delimit Semantic Fields. In particular, the recognition of the linguistic game in which words are typically formulated can be used as a criterion to identify classes of words composing lexical fields. The main problem of this assumption is that it is not clear how to distinguish linguistic games between each other. In fact, linguistic games are related by a complex network of similarities, but it is not possible to identify a set of discriminating features that allows us to univocally recognize them. "I can think of no better expression to characterize these similarities than 'family resemblances'; for the various resemblances between members of a family: build, features, color of eyes, gait, temperament, etc. etc. overlap and criss-cross in the same way. And I shall say: 'games' form a family" ([94], par. 67).

At first glance, the notion of linguistic game is no less obscure than those proposed by Weisgerber. The first relies on a fuzzy idea of family resemblance, the latter refer to some "external" relation with the real world. The main difference between those two visions is that the former can be investigated within the structuralist paradigm. In fact, we observe that linguistic games are naturally reflected in texts, allowing us to detect them from a word distribution analysis on a large scale corpus. In fact, according to Wittgenstein's view, the content of any text is located in a specific linguistic game, otherwise the text itself would be meaningless. Texts can be perceived as open windows through which we can observe the connections among concepts in the real world. Frequently co-occurring words in texts are then associated to the same linguistic game.

It follows that lexical fields can be identified from a corpus-based analysis of the lexicon, exploiting the connections between linguistic games and Semantic Fields already depicted. For example, the two words fork and glass are evidently in the same lexical field. A corpus-based analysis shows that they frequently co-occur in texts, then they are also related to the same linguistic game. On the other and, it is not clear what would be the relation among water and algorithm, if any. They are totally unrelated simply because the concrete situations (i.e. the linguistic games) in which they occur are in general distinct. It reflects the fact that they are often expressed in different texts, then they belong to different lexical fields.

Words in the same field can then be identified from a corpus-based analysis. In Sect. 2.6 we will describe in detail the lexical coherence assumption, that ensures the possibility of performing such a corpus-based acquisition process for lexical fields. Semantic Domains are basically Semantic Fields whose lexica show high lexical coherence.

Our proposal is then to merge the notion of linguistic game and that of Semantic Field, in order to provide an objective criterion to distinguish and delimit lexical fields from a corpus-based analysis of lexical co-occurences in texts. We refer to this particular view on Semantic Fields by using the name Semantic Domains. The concept of Semantic Domain is the main topic of this work, and it will be illustrated more formally in the following section.

2.3 Semantic Domains

In our usage, Semantic Domains are common areas of human discussion, such as ECONOMICS, POLITICS, LAW, SCIENCE, etc. (see Tab. 2.2), which demonstrate lexical coherence. Semantic Domains are Semantic Fields, characterized by sets of *domain words*, which often occur in texts about the corresponding domain. Semantic Domains can be automatically identified by exploiting a *lexical coherence* property manifested by texts in any natural language, and can be profitably used to structure a semantic network to define a computational lexicon.

As well as Semantic Fields, Semantic Domains correspond to both lexical fields and conceptual fields. In addition, the lexical coherence assumption allows us to represent Semantic Domains by sets of domain-specific text collections.[2] The symmetricalness of these three levels of representation, allows us to work at the preferred one. Throughout this book we will mainly adopt a lexical representation because it presents several advantages from a computational point of view.

Words belonging to lexical fields are called domain words. A substantial portion of the language terminology is characterized by domain words, whose meaning refers to lexical concepts belonging to the specific domains. Domain words are disambiguated when they are collocated into domain-specific texts by simply considering domain information [32].

Semantic Domains play a dual role in linguistic description. One role is characterizing word senses (i.e. *lexical concepts*), typically by assigning domain labels to word senses in a dictionary or lexicon (e.g. crane has senses in the domains of ZOOLOGY and CONSTRUCTION).[3] A second role is to characterize

[2] The textual interpretation motivates our usage of the term "Domain". In fact, this term is often used in Computational Linguistics either to refer to a collection of texts regarding a specific argument, as for example BIOMEDICINE, or to refer to ontologies describing a specific task.

[3] The WORDNET DOMAINS lexical resource is an extension of WORDNET which provides such domain labels for all synsets [56].

texts, typically as a generic level of Text Categorization (e.g. for classifying news and articles) [80].

At the lexical level Semantic Domains identify clusters of (domain) related lexical-concepts. i.e. sets of domain words. For example the concepts of `dog` and `mammal`, belonging to the domain ZOOLOGY, are related by the **is_a** relation. The same hold for many other concepts belonging to the same domain, as for example `soccer` and `sport`. On the other hand, it is quite infrequent to find semantic relations among concepts belonging to different domains, as for example `computer_graphics` and `mammifer`. In this sense Semantic Domains are shallow models for Semantic Fields: even if deeper semantic relations among lexical concepts are not explicitly identified, Semantic Domains provide a useful methodology to identify a class of strongly associated concepts. Domain relations are then crucial to identify ontological relations among terms from corpora (i.e. to induce automatically structured Semantic Fields, whose concepts are internally related).

At a text level domains are cluster of texts regarding similar topics/subjects. They can be perceived as collections of domain-specific texts, in which a generic corpus is organized. Examples of Semantic Domains at the text level are the subject taxonomies adopted to organize books in libraries, as for example the Dewey Decimal Classification [14] (see Sect. 2.5).

From a practical point of view, Semantic Domains have been considered as lists of related terms describing a particular subject or area of interest. In fact, term-based representations for Semantic Domains are quite easy to be obtained, e.g. by exploiting well consolidated and efficient shallow parsing techniques [36]. A disadvantage of term-based representations is lexical ambiguity: polysemous terms denote different lexical concepts in different domains, making it impossible to associate the term itself to one domain or the other. Anyway, term-based representations are effective, because most of the domain words are not ambiguous, allowing us to biunivocally associate terms and concepts in most of the relevant cases.

Domain words are typically highly correlated within texts, i.e. they tend to co-occur inside the same types of texts. The possibility of detecting such words from text collections is guaranteed by a *lexical coherence* property manifested by almost all the texts expressed in any natural language, i.e. the property of words belonging to the same domain to frequently co-occur in the same texts.[4]

Thus, Semantic Domains are a key concept in Computational Linguistics because they allow us to design a set of totally automatic corpus-based acquisition strategies, aiming to infer shallow Domain Models (see Chap. 3) to be exploited for further elaborations (e.g. ontology learning, text indexing, NLP systems). In addition, the possibility of automatically acquiring Semantic Domains from corpora is attractive both from an applicative and theoretical

[4] Note that the lexical coherence assumption is formulated here at a term level as an approximation of the strongest original claim that holds at the concept level.

point of view, because it allows us to design algorithms that can fit easily domain-specific problems while preserving their generality.

The next sections discuss two fundamental issues that arise when dealing with Semantic Domains in Computational Linguistics: (i) how to choose an appropriate partition for Semantic Domains; and (ii) how to define an adequate computational model to represent them. The first question is both an ontological and a practical issue, that requires us to take a (typically arbitrary and subjective) decision about the set of the relevant domain distinctions and their granularity. In order to answer the second question, it is necessary to define a computational model expressing domain relations among text, terms or concepts. In the following two sections we will address both problems.

2.4 The Domain Set

The problem of selecting an appropriate *domain set* is controversial. The particular choice of a domain set affects the way in which topic-proximity relations are set up, because it should be used to describe both semantic classes of texts and semantic classes of strongly related lexical concepts (i.e. domain concepts). An approximation of a lexical model for Semantic Domains can be easily obtained by clustering terms instead of concepts, assuming that most of the domain words are not ambiguous. At the text level Semantic Domains look like text archives, in which documents are categorized according to predefined taxonomies.

In this section, we discuss the problem of finding an adequate domain set, by proposing a set of "ideal" requirements to be satisfied by any domain set, aiming to reduce as much as possible the inherent level subjectivity required to perform this operation, while avoiding long-standing and useless ontological discussions. According to our experience, the following three criteria seem to be relevant to select an adequate set of domains:

Completeness: The domain set should be *complete*; i.e. all the possible texts/ concepts that can be expressed in the language should be assigned to at least one domain.

Balancement: The domain set should be *balanced*; i.e. the number of text/ concepts belonging to each domain should be uniformly distributed.

Separability: Semantic Domains should be *separable*, i.e. the same text/concept cannot be associated to more than one domain

The requirements stated below are formulated symmetrically at both the lexical and the text levels, imposing restrictions on the same domain set. This symmetrical view is intuitively reasonable. In fact, the larger the document collection, the larger its vocabulary. An unbalanced domain set at the text level will then reflect on an unbalanced domain set at the lexical level, and vice versa. The same holds for the separability requirement: if two domains overlap at the textual level then their overlapping will be reflected at the lexical level. An analogous argument can be made regarding completeness.

Unfortunately the requirements stated below should be perceived as "ideal" conditions, that in practice cannot be fully satisfied. They are based on the assumption that the language can be analyzed and represented in its totality, while in practice, and probably even theoretically, it is not possible to accept such an assumption for several reasons. We try to list them below:

- It seems quite difficult to define a truly complete domain set (i.e. general enough to represent any possible aspect of human knowledge), because it is simply impossible to collect a corpus that contains a set of documents representing the whole of human activity.
- The balancement requirement cannot be formulated without any "a-priori" estimation of the relevance of each domain in the language. One possibility is to select the domain set in a way that the size of each domain-specific text collection is uniform. In this case the set of domains will be balanced with respect to the corpus, but what about the balancement of the corpus itself?
- A certain degree of domain overlapping seems to be inevitable, since many domains are very intimately related (e.g. texts belonging to Mathematics and Physics are often hard to distinguish for non-experts, even if most of them agree on separating the two domains).

The only way to escape from the problem of subjectivity in the selection of a domain set is to restrict our attention to both the lexicon and the texts contained in an available corpus, hoping that the distribution of the texts in it would reflect the "true" domain distribution we want to model. Even if from a theoretical point of view it is impossible to find a truly representative corpus, from an applicative point of view corpus-based approaches allows us to automatically infer the required domain distinctions, representing most of the relevant information required to perform the particular NLP task.

2.5 WordNet Domains

In this section we describe WordNet Domains,[5] an extension of WordNet [25], in which each synset is annotated with one or more domain labels.

The domain set of WordNet Domains is composed of about 200 domain labels, selected from a number of dictionaries and then structured in a taxonomy according to their position in the (much larger) Dewey Decimal Classification system (DDC), which is commonly used for classifying books in libraries. DDC was chosen because it ensures good coverage, is easily available and is commonly used to classify "text material" by librarians. Finally, it is

[5] Freely available for research from `http://wndomains.itc.it`.

officially documented and the interpretation of each domain is detailed in the reference manual [14].[6]

Table 2.1. WordNet Domains annotation for the senses of the noun "bank"

Sense	Synset and Gloss	Domains	Semcor
#1	depository financial institution, bank, banking concern, banking company (a financial institution...)	Economy	20
#2	bank (sloping land...)	Geography, Geology	14
#3	bank (a supply or stock held in reserve...)	Economy	
#4	bank, bank building (a building...)	Architecture, Economy	
#5	bank (an arrangement of similar objects...)	Factotum	1
#6	savings bank, coin bank, money box, bank (a container...)	Economy	
#7	bank (a long ridge or pile...)	Geography, Geology	2
#8	bank (the funds held by a gambling house...)	Economy, Play	
#9	bank, cant, camber (a slope in the turn of a road...)	Architecture	
#10	bank (a flight maneuver...)	Transport	

Domain labeling of synsets is complementary to the information already in WordNet. First, a domain may include synsets of different syntactic categories: for instance Medicine groups together senses of nouns, such as `doctor#1` and `hospital#1`, and from verbs, such as `operate#7`. Second, a domain may include senses from different WordNet sub-hierarchies (i.e derived from different "unique beginners" or from different "lexicographer files"[7]). For example, Sport contains senses such as `athlete#1`, derived from `life_form#1`, `game_equipment#1` from `physical_object#1`, `sport#1` from `act#2`, and `playing field#1` from `location#1`.

The annotation methodology [56] was primarily manual and was based on lexicon-semantic criteria that take advantage of existing conceptual relations in WordNet. First, a small number of high level synsets were man-

[6] In a separate work [7] the requirements expressed in Sect. 2.4 were tested on the domain set provided by the first distribution of WordNet Domains, concluding that they have been partially respected. In the same paper a different taxonomy is proposed to alleviate some unbalancement problems that have been found in the previous version.

[7] The noun hierarchy is a tree forest, with several roots (*unique beginners*). The *lexicographer files* are the source files from which WordNet is "compiled". Each lexicographer file is usually related to a particular topic.

ually annotated with their pertinent domain. Then, an automatic procedure exploited some of the WORDNET relations (i.e. hyponymy, troponymy, meronymy, antonymy and pertain-to) to extend the manual assignments to all the reachable synsets. For example, this procedure labeled the synset {`beak, bill, neb, nib`} with the code ZOOLOGY through inheritance from the synset {`bird`}, following a **part-of** relation. However, there are cases in which the inheritance procedure was blocked, by inserting "exceptions", to prevent incorrect propagation. For instance, `barber_chair#1`, being a **part-of** `barbershop#1`, which in turn is annotated with COMMERCE, would wrongly inherit the same domain. The entire process had cost approximately two person-years.

Domains may be used to group together senses of a particular word that have the same domain labels. Such grouping reduces the level of word ambiguity when disambiguating to a domain, as demonstrated in Table 2.1. The noun `bank` has ten different senses in WORDNET 1.6: three of them (i.e. `bank#1`, `bank#3` and `bank#6`) can be grouped under the ECONOMY domain, while `bank#2` and `bank#7` belong to both GEOGRAPHY and GEOLOGY. Grouping related senses in order to achieve more "practical" coarse-grained senses is an emerging topic in WSD [71].

In our experiments, we adopted only the domain set reported in Table 2.2, relabeling each synset with the most specific ancestor in the WORDNET DOMAINS hierarchy included in this set. For example, SPORT is used instead of VOLLEY or BASKETBALL, which are subsumed by SPORT. This subset was selected empirically to allow a sensible level of abstraction without losing much relevant information, overcoming data sparseness for less frequent domains.

Some WORDNET synsets do not belong to a specific domain but rather correspond to general language and may appear in any context. Such senses are tagged in WORDNET DOMAINS with a FACTOTUM label, which may be considered as a "placeholder" for all other domains. Accordingly, FACTOTUM is not one of the dimensions in our Domain Vectors (see Sect. 2.7), but is rather reflected as a property of those vectors which have a relatively uniform distribution across all domains.

2.6 Lexical Coherence: A Bridge from the Lexicon to the Texts

In this section we describe into detail the concept of *lexical coherence*, reporting a set of experiments we made to demonstrate this assumption. To perform our experiments we used the lexical resource WORDNET DOMAINS and a large scale sense tagged corpus of English texts: SemCor [51], the portion of the Brown corpus semantically annotated with WORDNET senses.

The basic hypothesis of lexical coherence is that a great percentage of the concepts expressed in the same text belongs to the same domain. Lexical

Table 2.2. Domains distribution over WORDNET synsets

Domain	#Syn	Domain	#Syn	Domain	#Syn
Factotum	36820	Biology	21281	Earth	4637
Psychology	3405	Architecture	3394	Medicine	3271
Economy	3039	Alimentation	2998	Administration	2975
Chemistry	2472	Transport	2443	Art	2365
Physics	2225	Sport	2105	Religion	2055
Linguistics	1771	Military	1491	Law	1340
History	1264	Industry	1103	Politics	1033
Play	1009	Anthropology	963	Fashion	937
Mathematics	861	Literature	822	Engineering	746
Sociology	679	Commerce	637	Pedagogy	612
Publishing	532	Tourism	511	Computer_Science	509
Telecommunication	493	Astronomy	477	Philosophy	381
Agriculture	334	Sexuality	272	Body_Care	185
Artisanship	149	Archaeology	141	Veterinary	92
Astrology	90				

coherence allows us to disambiguate ambiguous words, by associating domain-specific senses to them. Lexical coherence is then a basic property of most of the texts expressed in any natural language. Otherwise stated, words taken out of context show domain polysemy, but, when they occur into real texts, their polysemy is solved by the relations among their senses and the domain-specific concepts occurring in their contests.

Intuitively, texts may exhibit somewhat stronger or weaker orientation towards specific domains, but it seems less sensible to have a text that is not related to at least one domain. In other words, it is difficult to find a "generic" (FACTOTUM) text. The same assumption is not valid for terms. In fact, the most frequent terms in the language, that constitute the greatest part of the tokens in texts, are generic terms, that are not associated to any domain.

This intuition is largely supported by our data: all the texts in SemCor exhibit concepts belonging to a small number of relevant domains, demonstrating the domain coherence of the lexical concepts expressed in the same text. In [59] a "one domain per discourse hypothesis" was proposed and verified on SemCor. This observation fits with the general lexical coherence assumption.

The availability of WORDNET DOMAINS makes it possible to analyze the content of a text in terms of domain information. Two related aspects will be addressed. Section 2.6 proposes a test to estimate the number of words in a text that brings relevant domain information. Section 2.6 reports on an experiment whose aim is to verify the "one domain per discourse" hypothesis. These experiments make use of the SemCor corpus.

We will show that the property of lexical coherence allows us to define corpus-based acquisition strategies for acquiring domain information, for example by detecting classes of related terms from classes of domain related texts. On the other hand, lexical coherence allows us to identify classes of domain related texts starting from domain-specific terms. The consistency among the textual and the lexical representation of Semantic Domains allows us to define a "dual" *Domain Space*, in which terms, concepts and texts can be represented and compared.

Domain Words in Texts

The lexical coherence assumption claims that most of the concepts in texts belongs to the same domain. The experiment reported in this section aims to demonstrate that this assumption holds into real texts, by counting the percentage of words that actually share the same domain in them.

We observed that words in a text do not behave homogeneously as far as domain information is concerned. In particular, we have identified three classes of words:

- *Text Related Domain words (TRD)*: words that have at least one sense that contributes to determine the domain of the whole text; for instance, the word bank in a text concerning ECONOMY is likely to be a text related domain word.
- *Text Unrelated Domain words (TUD)*: words that have senses belonging to specific domains (i.e. they are non-generic words) but do not contribute to the domain of the text; for instance, the occurrence of church in a text about ECONOMY does not probably affect the whole topic of the text.
- *Text Unrelated Generic words (TUG)*: words that do not bring relevant domain information at all (i.e. the majority of their senses are annotated with FACTOTUM); for instance, a verb like to be is likely to fall in this class, whatever the domain of the whole text.

In order to provide a quantitative estimation of the distribution of the three word classes, an experiment has been carried out on the SemCor corpus using WORDNET DOMAINS as a repository for domain annotations. In the experiment we considered 42 domains labels (FACTOTUM was not included). For each text in SemCor, all the domains were scored according to their frequency among the senses of the words in the text. The three top scoring domains are considered as the prevalent domains in the text. These domains have been calculated for the whole text, without taking into account possible domain variations that can occur within portions of the text. Then each word of a text has been assigned to one of the three classes according to the fact that (i) at least one domain of the word is present in the three prevalent domains of the text (i.e. a TRD word); (ii) the majority of the senses of the word have a domain but none of them belongs to the top three of the text (i.e. a TUD word); (iii) the majority of the senses of the word are FACTOTUM and none of the other senses belongs to the top three domains of the text (i.e. a TUG word). Then each group of words has been further analyzed by part of speech and the average polysemy with respect of WORDNET has been calculated.

Table 2.3. Word distribution in SemCor according to the prevalent domains of the texts

Word class	Nouns	Verbs	Adjectives	Adverbs	All
TRD words	18,732 (34.5%)	2416 (8.7%)	1982 (9.6%)	436 (3.7%)	21%
Polysemy	3.90	9.55	4.17	1.62	4.46
TUD words	13,768 (25.3%)	2224 (8.1%)	815 (3.9%)	300 (2.5%)	15%
Polysemy	4.02	7.88	4.32	1.62	4.49
TUG words	21,902 (40.2%)	22,933 (83.2%)	17,987 (86.5%)	11,131 (93.8%)	64%
Polysemy	5.03	10.89	4.55	2.78	6.39

Results, reported in Table 2.3, show that a substantial quantity of words (21%) in texts actually carry domain information which is compatible with the prevalent domains of the whole text, with a significant (34.5%) contribution of nouns. TUG words (i.e. words whose senses are tagged with FACTOTUM) are, as expected, both the most frequent (i.e. 64%) and the most polysemous words in the text. This is especially true for verbs (83.2%), which often have generic meanings that do not contribute to determine the domain of the text. It is worthwhile to notice here that the percentage of TUD is lower than the percentage of TRD, even if it contain all the words belonging to the remaining 39 domains.

In summary, a great percentage of words inside texts tends to share the same domain, demonstrating lexical coherence. Coherence is higher for nouns, which constitute the largest part of the domain words in the lexicon.

One Domain per Discourse

The One Sense per Discourse (OSD) hypothesis puts forward the idea that there is a strong tendency for multiple uses of a word to share the same sense in a well-written discourse. Depending on the methodology used to calculate OSD, [26] claims that OSD is substantially verified (98%), while [49], using WORDNET as a sense repository, found that 33% of the words in SemCor have more than one sense within the same text, basically invalidating OSD.

Following the same line, a One Domain per Discourse (ODD) hypothesis would claim that multiple uses of a word in a coherent portion of text tend to share the same domain. If demonstrated, ODD would reinforce the main hypothesis of this work, i.e. that the prevalent domain of a text is an important feature for selecting the correct sense of the words in that text.

To support ODD an experiment has been carried out using WORDNET DOMAINS as a repository for domain information. We applied to domain labels the same methodology proposed by [49] to calculate sense variation: it is sufficient for just one occurrence of a word in the same text with different meanings to invalidate the OSD hypothesis. A set of 23,877 ambiguous words with multiple occurrences in the same document in SemCor was extracted and the number of words with multiple sense assignments was counted. Sem-

Table 2.4. One sense per discourse vs. one domain per discourse

Pos	Tokens	Exceptions to OSD	Exceptions to ODD
All	23,877	7469 (31%)	2466 (10%)
Nouns	10,291	2403 (23%)	1142 (11%)
Verbs	6658	3154 (47%)	916 (13%)
Adjectives	4495	1100 (24%)	391 (9%)
Adverbs	2336	790 (34%)	12 (1%)

cor senses for each word were mapped to their corresponding domains in WORDNET DOMAINS and for each occurrence of the word the intersection among domains was considered. To understand the difference between OSD and ODD, let us suppose that the word bank (see Table 2.1) occurs three times in the text with three different senses (e.g. bank#1, bank#3, bank#8). This case would invalidate OSD but would be consistent with ODD because the intersection among the corresponding domains is not empty (i.e. the domain ECONOMY).

Results of the experiment, reported in Table 2.4, show that ODD is verified, corroborating the hypothesis that lexical coherence is an essential feature of texts (i.e. there are only a few relevant domains in a text). Exceptions to ODD (10% of word occurrences) might be due to *domain variations* within SemCor texts, which are quite long (about 2000 words). In these cases the same word can belong to different domains in different portions of the same text. Figure 2.2, generated after having disambiguated all the words in the text with respect to their possible domains, shows how the relevance of two domains, PEDAGOGY and SPORT, varies through a single text. Domain relevance is defined in Sect. 3.1.

As a consequence, the idea of "relevant domain" actually makes sense within a portion of text (i.e. a context), rather than with respect to the whole text. This also affects WSD. Suppose, for instance, the word acrobatics (third sentence in Fig. 2.2) has to be disambiguated. It would seem reasonable to choose an appropriate sense considering the domain of a portion of text around the word, rather than relevant for the whole text. In the example the local relevant domain is SPORT, which would correctly cause the selection of the first sense of acrobatics.

2.7 Computational Models for Semantic Domains

Any computational model for Semantic Domain is asked to represent the domain relations in at least one of the following (symmetric) levels.

Text level: Domains are represented by relations among texts.
Concept level: Domains are represented by relations among lexical concepts.
Term level: Domains are represented by relations among terms.

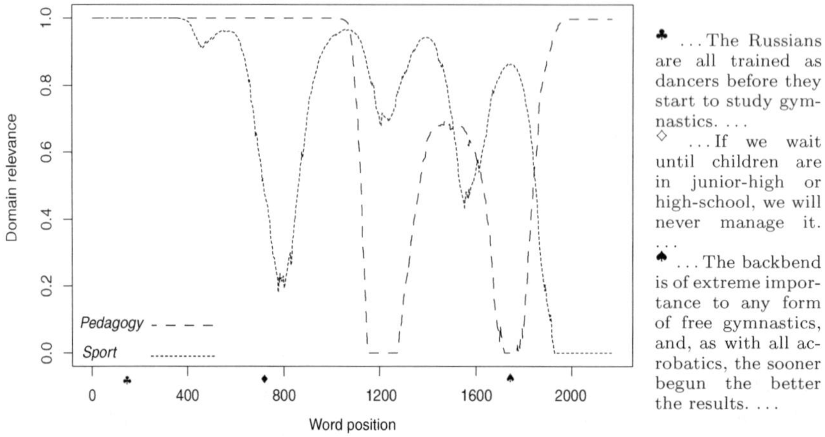

Fig. 2.2. Domain variation in the text `br-e24` from the SemCor corpus

It is not necessary to explicitly define a domain model for all those levels, because they are symmetric. In fact it is possible to establish automatic procedures to transfer domain information from one to the other level, exploiting the lexical-coherence assumption. Below we report some attempts we found in the Computational Linguistics literature to represent Semantic Domains.

Concept Annotation

Semantic Domains can be described at a concept level by annotating lexical concepts into a lexical resource [56]. Many dictionaries, as for example LDOCE [76], indicate domain-specific usages by attaching Subject Field Codes to word senses. The domain annotation provides a natural way to group lexical concepts into semantic clusters, allowing us to reduce the granularity of the sense discrimination. In Sect. 2.5 we have described WordNet Domains, a large scale lexical resource in which lexical concepts are annotated by domain labels.

Text Annotation

Semantic Domains can be described at a text level by annotating texts according to a set of Semantic Domains or categories. This operation is implicit when annotated corpora are provided to train Text Categorization systems. Recently, a large scale corpus, annotated by adopting the domain set of WordNet Domains, is being created at ITC-irst, in the framework of the EU-funded MEANING project.[8] Its novelty consists in the fact that domain-representativeness has been chosen as the fundamental criterion for the selection of the texts to be included in the corpus. A core set of 42 basic domains,

[8] `http://www.lsi.upc.es/`*sim*`nlp/meaning/documentation/`.

broadly covering all the branches of knowledge, has been chosen to be represented in the corpus. Even if the corpus is not yet complete, it is the first lexical resource explicitly developed with the goal of studying the domain relations between the lexicon and texts.

Topic Signatures

The topic-specific context models (i.e. neighborhoods) as constructed by [35] can be viewed as signatures of the topic in question. They are sets of words that can be used to identify the topic (i.e. the domain, in our terminology) in which the described linguistic entity is typically located.

However, a topic signature can be constructed even without the use of subject codes by generating it (semi-)automatically from a lexical resource and then validating it on topic-specific corpora [38]. An extension of this idea is to construct "topics" around individual senses of a word by automatically retrieving a number of documents corresponding to this sense. The collected documents then represent a 'topic out of which a topic signature may be extracted, which in turn corresponds directly to the initial word sense under investigation. This approach has been adopted in [1].

Topic signatures for sense can be perceived as a computational model for Semantic Domains, because they relate senses co-occurring with a set of lexically coherent terms. Topic signatures allows us to detect domain relations among concepts, avoiding taking any a-priori decision about a set of relevant domains. In addition topic signatures provide a viable way to relate lexical concepts to texts, as required for any computational model for Semantic Domain.

Finally, topic signatures can be associated to texts and terms, adopting similar strategies, allowing us to compare those different objects, so to transfer domain information from one level to the other.

Domain Vectors

Semantic Domains can be used to define a vectorial space, namely the *Domain Space* (see Sect. 3.3), in which terms, texts and concepts can be represented together. Each domain is represented by a different dimension, and any linguistic entity is represented by means of Domain Vectors (DVs) defined in this space. The value of each component of a DV is the domain relevance (see Sect. 3.1) estimated between the object and the corresponding domain.

Typically, DVs related to generic senses (namely FACTOTUM concepts) have a flat distribution, while DVs for domain-specific senses are strongly oriented along one dimension. As is common for vector representations, DVs enable us to compute domain similarity between objects of either the same or different types using the same similarity metric, defined in a common vectorial space. This property suggests the potential of utilizing domain similarity between various types of objects for different NLP tasks. For example, measuring the similarity between the DV of a word context and the DVs of its alternative senses is useful for WSD.

3

Domain Models

In this chapter we introduce the Domain Model (DM), a computational model for Semantic Domains that we used to represent domain information for our applications. DMs describe domain relations at the term level (see Sect. 2.7), and are exploited to estimate topic similarity among texts and terms. In spite of their simplicity, DMs represent lexical ambiguity and variability, and can be derived either from the lexical resource WORDNET DOMAINS (see Sect. 2.5) or by performing term clustering operations on large corpora. In our implementation, term clustering is performed by means of a Latent Semantic Analysis (LSA) of the term-by-document matrix representing a large corpus.

The approach we have defined to estimate topic similarity by exploiting DMs consists of defining a Domain Space, in which texts, concepts and terms, described by means of DVs, can be represented and then compared. The Domain Space improves the "traditional" methodology adopted to estimate text similarity, based on a VSM representation. In fact, in the Domain Space external knowledge provided by the DM is used to estimate the similarity of novel texts, taking into account second-order relations among words inferred from a large corpus.

3.1 Domain Models: Definition

A DM is a computational model for Semantic Domains, that represents domain information at the term level, by defining a set of term clusters. Each cluster represents a Semantic Domain, i.e. a set of terms that often co-occur in texts having similar topics. A DM is represented by a $k \times k'$ rectangular matrix $\mathbf{D}$, containing the domain relevance for each term with respect to each domain, as illustrated in Table 3.1.

More formally, let $\mathcal{D} = \{D_1, D_2, ..., D_{k'}\}$ be a set of domains. A DM is fully defined by a $k \times k'$ matrix $\mathbf{D}$ representing in each cell $\mathbf{d_{i,z}}$ the *domain relevance* of term w_i with respect to the domain D_z, where k is the vocabulary size. The domain relevance $R(D_z, o)$ of a domain D_z with respect to a linguistic

A. Gliozzo and C. Strapparava, *Semantic Domains in Computational Linguistics*,
DOI: 10.1007/978-3-540-68158-8_3, © Springer-Verlag Berlin Heidelberg 2009

Table 3.1. Example of Domain Model

	MEDICINE	COMPUTER_SCIENCE
HIV	1	0
AIDS	1	0
virus	0.5	0.5
laptop	0	1

object o – text, term or concept – gives a measure of the association degree between D and o. $R(D_z, o)$ gets real values, where a higher value indicates a higher degree of relevance. In most of our settings the relevance value ranges in the interval $[0, 1]$, but this is not a necessary requirement.

DMs can be used to describe lexical ambiguity and variability. *Ambiguity* is represented by associating one term to more than one domain, while *variability* is represented by associating different terms to the same domain. For example the term `virus` is associated to both the domain COMPUTER_SCIENCE and the domain MEDICINE (ambiguity) while the domain MEDICINE is associated to both the terms `AIDS` and `HIV` (variability).

The main advantage of representing Semantic Domains at the term level is that the vocabulary size is in general bounded, while the number of texts in a corpus can be, in principle, unlimited. As far as the memory requirements are concerned, representing domain information at the lexical level is evidently the cheapest solution, because it requires a fixed amount of memory even if large scale corpora have to be processed.

A DM can be estimated either from hand made lexical resources such as WORDNET DOMAINS [56] (see Sect. 3.4), or by performing a term clustering process on a large corpus (see Sect. 3.5). The second methodology is more attractive, because it allows us to automatically acquire DMs for different languages. A DM can be used to define a Domain Space (see Sect. 3.2), a vectorial space where both terms and texts can be represented and compared. This space improves over the traditional VSM by introducing second-order relations among terms during the topic similarity estimation.

3.2 The Vector Space Model

The recent success obtained by Information Retrieval (IR) and Text Categorization (TC) systems supports the claim that topic similarity among texts can be estimated by simply comparing their Bag-of-Words (BoW) feature representations.[1] It has also been demonstrated that richer feature sets, as for example syntactic features [67], do not improve the system performance, confirming our claim. Another well established result is that not all the terms

[1] BoW features for a text are expressed by the unordered lists of its term.

have the same descriptiveness with respect to a certain domain or topic. This is the case of very frequent words, such as and, is and have, that are often eliminated from the feature representation of texts, as well as very infrequent words, usually called *hapax legomena* (lit. "said only once"). In fact, the former are spread uniformly among most of the texts (i.e. they are not associated to any domain), the latter are often spelling errors or neologisms that have not been yet lexicalized.

A geometrical way to express BoW features is the *Vector Space Model* (VSM): texts are represented by feature vectors expressing the frequency of each term in a lexicon, then they are compared by exploiting vector similarity metrics, such as the dot product or the cosine. More formally, let $\mathcal{T} = \{t_1, t_2, \ldots, t_n\}$ be a corpus, let $V = \{w_1, w_2, \ldots, w_k\}$ be its vocabulary, let $\mathbf{T}$ be the $k \times n$ term-by-document matrix representing $\mathcal{T}$, such that $\mathbf{t}_{i,j}$ is the frequency of word w_i into the text t_j. The VSM is a k-dimensional space $\mathbf{R}^k$, in which the text $t_j \in \mathcal{T}$ is represented by means of the vector $\mathbf{t_j}$ such that the ith component of $\mathbf{t}_j$ is $\mathbf{t}_{i,j}$, as illustrated by Fig. 3.1. The similarity among two texts in the VSM is estimated by computing the cosine among their corresponding vectors. In the VSM, the text $t_i \in T$ is represented by means of the ith column vector of the matrix $\mathbf{T}$.

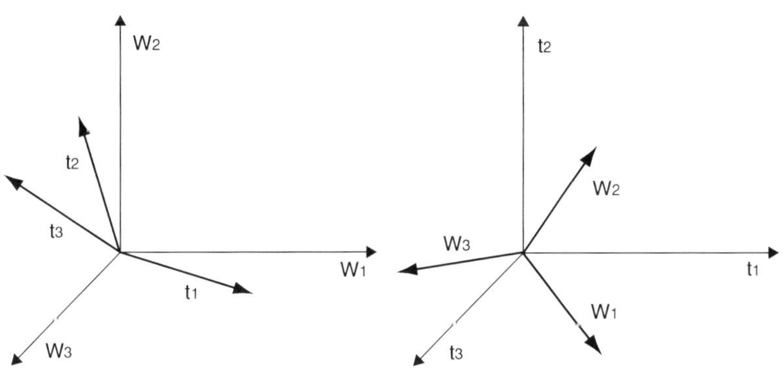

Fig. 3.1. The Text VSM (left) and the Term VSM (right) are two disjointed vectorial spaces

A similar model can be defined to estimate term similarity. In this case, terms are represented by means of feature vectors expressing the texts in which they occur in a corpus. In the rest of this book we will adopt the expression *Term VSM* to denote this space, while the expression *Text VSM* refers to the geometric representation for texts. The *Term VSM* is then a vectorial space having one dimension for each text in the corpus.

More formally, the term VSM is a n-dimensional space $\mathbf{R}^n$, in which the term $w_i \in \mathcal{V}$ is represented by means of the vector $\mathbf{w_i}$ such that the jth component of $\mathbf{w}_i$ is $\mathbf{t}_{i,j}$ (see Fig. 3.1). As for the Text VSM, the similarity between two terms is estimated by the dot product or the cosine between their corresponding vectors. The domain relations among terms are then detected by analyzing their co-occurrence in a corpus. This operation is motivated by the lexical coherence assumption, which guarantees that most of the terms in the same text belong to the same domain: co-occurring terms in texts have a good chance to show domain relations.

Even if, at first glance, the Text and the Term VSMs appear symmetric, their properties radically differ. In fact, one of the consequences of Zipf's laws [100] is that the vocabulary size of a corpus becomes stable when the corpus size increases. It means that the dimensionality of the Text VSM is bounded to the number of terms in the language, while the dimensionality of the Term VSM is proportional to the corpus size. The Text VSM is then able to represent large scale corpora in a compact space, while the same is not true for Term VSM, leading to the paradox that the larger the corpus size, the worse the similarity estimation in this space. Another difference between the two spaces is that it is not clear how to perform feature selection on the Term VSM, while it is a common practice in IR to remove irrelevant terms (e.g. stop words, hapaxes) from the document index, in order to keep the dimensionality of the feature space low. In fact, it is nonsense to say that some texts have higher discriminative power than others because, as discussed in the previous section, any well written text should satisfy a lexical coherence assumption. Finally, the Text and the Term VSM are basically disjointed (i.e. they do not share any common dimension), making impossible a direct topic similarity estimation between a term and a text, as illustrated by Fig. 3.1.

3.3 The Domain Space

Both the Text and the Term VSM are affected by several problems. The Text VSM is not able to deal with lexical *variability* and *ambiguity* (see Sect. 1.1). For example, the two sentences "*he is affected by AIDS*" and "*HIV is a virus*" do not have any words in common. In the Text VSM their similarity is zero because they have orthogonal vectors, even if the concepts they express are very closely related. On the other hand, the similarity between the two sentences "*the laptop has been infected by a virus*" and "*HIV is a virus*" would turn out very high, due to the ambiguity of the word `virus`. The main limitation of the term VSM is feature *sparseness*. As long as domain relations have to be modeled, we are mainly interested in domain-specific words. Such words are often infrequent in corpora, then they are represented by means of very sparse vectors in the Term VSM. Most of the similarity estimations among domain-specific words would turn out null, with the effect of producing non-meaningful similarity assignments for the more interesting terms.

In the literature several approaches have been proposed to overcome such limitations: the Generalized VSM [95], distributional clusters [5], concept-based representations [34] and Latent Semantic Indexing [22]. Our proposal is to define a Domain Space, a cluster-based representation that can be used to estimate term and text similarity.

The Domain Space is a vectorial space in which both terms and text can be represented and compared. Once a DM has been defined by the matrix $\mathbf{D}$, the Domain Space is a k' dimensional space, in which both texts and terms are represented by means of DVs, i.e. vectors representing the domain relevances among the linguistic object and each domain. The term vector $\mathbf{w}'_i$ for the term $w_i \in \mathcal{V}$ in the Domain Space is the ith row of $\mathbf{D}$. The DV $\mathbf{t}'$ for the text t is obtained by the following linear transformation, that projects it from the Text VSM into the Domain Space:

$$\mathbf{t}'_\mathbf{j} = \mathbf{t}_\mathbf{j}(\mathbf{I}^{\mathrm{IDF}}\mathbf{D}) \tag{3.1}$$

where $\mathbf{I}^{\mathrm{IDF}}$ is a diagonal matrix such that $i^{\mathrm{IDF}}_{i,i} = \mathrm{IDF}(w_i)$, $\mathbf{t}_j$ is represented as a row vector, and $IDF(w_i)$ is the *Inverse Document Frequency* of w_i. The similarity among DVs in the Domain Space is estimated by means of the cosine operation.[2]

In the Domain Space the vectorial representation of terms and documents are "augmented" by the hidden underlying network of domain relations represented in the DM, providing a richer model for lexical understanding and topic similarity estimation. When compared in the Domain Space, texts and terms are projected in a cognitive space, in which their representations are much more expressive. The structure of the Domain Space can be perceived as segmentation of the original VSMs into a set of relevant clusters of similar terms and documents providing a richer feature representation to texts and terms for topic similarity estimation.

Geometrically, the Domain Space is illustrated in Fig. 3.2. Both terms and texts are represented in a common vectorial space having lower dimensionality. In this space a uniform comparison among them can be done, while in the classical VSMs this operation is not possible, as illustrated by Fig. 3.1.

The Domain Space allows us to reduce the impact of ambiguity and variability in the VSM, by inducing a non-sparse space where both texts and terms can be represented and compared. For example, the rows of the matrix reported in Table 3.1 contain the DVs for the terms HIV, AIDS, virus and laptop, expressed in a bidimensional space whose dimensions are MEDICINE and COMPUTER_SCIENCE. Exploiting the second-order relations among the terms expressed by that matrix, it is possible to assign a very high similarity to the two sentences "*He is affected by AIDS*" and "*HIV is a virus*", because the terms AIDS, HIV and virus are highly associated to the domain MEDICINE.

The Domain Space presents several advantages if compared to both the Text and the Term VSMs: (i) lower dimensionality, (ii) sparseness is avoided

---

[2] The Domain Space is a particular instance of the Generalized VSM, proposed in [95], where domain relations are exploited to define a mapping function. In the literature, this general schema has been proposed by using information from many different sources, as for example conceptual density in WORDNET [4].

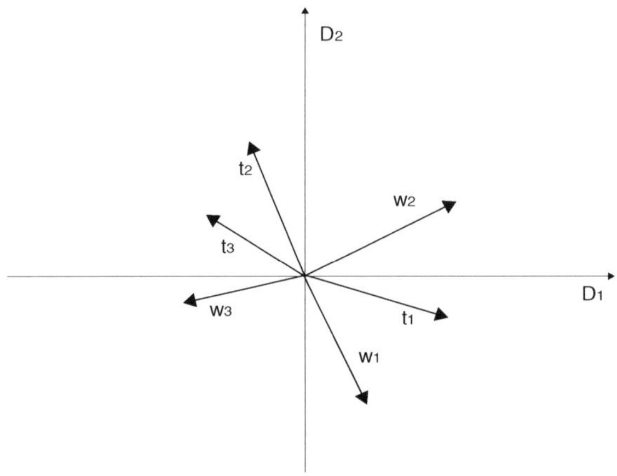

Fig. 3.2. Terms and texts in the Domain Space

(iii) duality. The third property, *duality*, is very interesting because it allows a direct and uniform estimation of the similarities among terms and the texts, an operation that cannot be performed in the classical VSM. The duality of the Domain Space is a crucial property for the Intensional Learning settings, in which it is required to classify texts according to a set of categories described by means of lists of terms.

In many tasks presented in the following chapters, we defined the Domain Kernel, a similarity function among terms and documents in the Domain Space that can be profitably used by many NLP applications. In the following sections we will describe two different methodologies to acquire DMs either from a lexical resource (see Sect. 3.4) or from an large corpus of untagged texts (see Sect. 3.5).

3.4 WordNet-Based Domain Models

A DM is fully specified whether a domain set is selected, and a domain relevance function among terms and domains is specified. The lexical resource WORDNET DOMAINS, described in Sect. 2.5, provide all the information required. Below we show how to use it to derive a DM.

Intuitively, a domain D is relevant for a concept c if D is relevant for the texts in which c usually occurs. As an approximation, the information in WORDNET DOMAINS can be used to estimate such a function. Let $\mathcal{D} = \{D_1, D_2, ..., D_{k'}\}$ be the domain set of WORDNET DOMAINS, let $C = \{c_1, c_2, ..., c_s\}$ be the set of concepts (synsets), let $senses(w) = \{c | c \in C, c \text{ is a sense of } w\}$ be the set of WORDNET synsets containing the word w and let $R : \mathcal{D} \times C \Rightarrow \mathbb{R}$ be the domain relevance function for concepts. The domain assignment to synsets from WORDNET DOMAINS is represented by the function $\mathrm{Dom}(c) \subseteq \mathcal{D}$, which returns the set of domains associated with each synset c. Formula 3.2 defines the domain relevance function:

$$R(D,c) = \begin{cases} 1/|\mathrm{Dom}(c)| & : \texttt{if } D \in \mathrm{Dom}(c) \\ 1/k' & : \texttt{if } \mathrm{Dom}(c) = \{\textsc{Factotum}\} \\ 0 & : \texttt{otherwise} \end{cases} \quad (3.2)$$

where k' is the domain set cardinality.

$R(D,c)$ can be perceived as an estimated prior for the probability of the domain given the concept, according to the WordNet Domains annotation. Under these settings Factotum (generic) concepts have uniform and low relevance values for each domain while domain oriented concepts have high relevance values for a particular domain. For example, given Table 2.1, $R(\textsc{Economy}, \texttt{bank\#5}) = 1/42$, $R(\textsc{Economy}, \texttt{bank\#1}) = 1$, and $R(\textsc{Economy}, \texttt{bank\#8}) = 1/2$.

This framework also provides a formal definition of *domain polysemy* for a word w, defined as the number of different domains belonging to w's senses: $P(w) = |\bigcup_{c \in senses(w)} Dom(c)|$. We propose using such a coarse grained sense distinction for WSD, enabling us to obtain higher accuracy for this easier task.

The domain relevance for a word is derived directly from the domain relevance values of its senses. Intuitively, a domain D is relevant for a word w if D is relevant for one or more senses c of w. Let $V = \{w_1, w_2, ...w_k\}$ be the vocabulary. The domain relevance for a word $R : \mathcal{D} \times V \Rightarrow \mathbb{R}$ is defined as the average relevance value of its senses:

$$R(D_i, w_z) = \frac{1}{|\mathrm{senses}(w_i)|} \sum_{c \in \mathrm{senses}(w_i)} R(D_z, c) \quad (3.3)$$

Notice that domain relevance for a monosemous word is equal to the relevance value of the corresponding concept. A word with several senses will be relevant for each of the domains of its senses, but with a lower value. Thus monosemic words are more domain oriented than polysemous ones and provide a greater amount of domain information. This phenomenon often converges with the common property of less frequent words being more informative, as they typically have fewer senses. The DM is finally defined by the $k \times k'$ matrix $\mathbf{D}$ such that $\mathbf{d_{i,j}} = R(D_j, w_i)$.

The WordNet-based DM presents several drawbacks, both from a theoretical and from an applicative point of view:

- The matrix $\mathbf{D}$ is fixed, and cannot be automatically adapted to the particular applicative needs.
- The domain set of WordNet Domains is far from complete, balanced and separated, as required in Sect. 2.4.
- The lexicon represented by the DM is limited, most of the domain-specific terms are not present in WordNet.

3.5 Corpus-Based Acquisition of Domain Models

To overcome the limitations we have found in the WordNet-based DMs, we propose the use of corpus-based acquisition techniques. In particular we want to acquire both the domain set and the domain relevance function in a fully automatic way, in order to avoid subjectivity and to define more flexible models that can be easily ported among different applicative domains without requiring any manual intervention.

Term Clustering techniques can be adopted to perform this operation. Clustering is the most important unsupervised learning problem. It deals with finding a structure in a collection of unlabeled data. It consists on organizing objects into groups whose members are similar in some way, and dissimilar to the objects belonging to other clusters. It is possible to distinguish between soft[3] and hard clustering techniques. In hard clustering, each object should be assigned to exactly one cluster, whereas in soft clustering it is more desirable to let an object be assigned to several. In general soft clustering techniques quantify the degree of association among each object and each cluster.

Clustering algorithms can be applied to a wide variety of objects. The operation of grouping terms according to their distributional properties in a corpus is called Term Clustering. Any Term Clustering algorithm can be used to induce a DM from a large scale corpus: each cluster is used to define a domain, and the degree of association between each term and each cluster, estimated by the learning algorithm, provide a domain relevance function. DMs are then naturally defined by soft-clusters of terms, that allows us to define fuzzy associations among terms and clusters.

When defining a clustering algorithm, it is very important to carefully select a set of relevant features to describe the objects, because different feature representations will lead to different groups of objects. In the literature, terms have been represented either by means of their association with other terms or by means of the documents in which they occur in the corpus (for an overview about term representation techniques see [17]). We prefer the second solution because it fits perfectly the lexical coherence assumption that lies at the basis of the concept of Semantic Domain: semantically related terms are those terms that co-occur in the same documents. For this reason we are more interested in clustering techniques working on the Term VSM.

In principle, any Term Clustering algorithm can be used to acquire a DM from a large corpus, as for example Fuzzy C-Means [11] and Information Bottleneck [86]. In the next section we will describe an algorithm based on Latent Semantic Analysis that can be used to perform this operation in a very efficient way.

[3] In the literature soft-clustering algorithms are also referred to by the term fuzzy clustering. For an overview see [37].

3.6 Latent Semantic Analysis for Term Clustering

Latent Semantic Analysis (LSA) is a very well known technique that has been originally developed to estimate the similarity among texts and terms in a corpus. In this section we exploit its basic assumptions to define the Text Clustering algorithm we used to acquire DMs for our experiments.

LSA is a method for extracting and representing the contextual-usage meaning of words by statistical computations applied to a large corpus [50]. Such contextual usages can be used instead of the word itself to represent texts. LSA is performed by projecting the vectorial representations of both terms and texts from the VSM into a common LSA space by means of a linear transformation.

The most basic way to perform LSA is to represent each term by means of its similarities with each text in a large corpus. Terms are represented in a vectorial space having one component for each text, i.e. in the Term VSM. The space determined in such a way is a particular instance of the Domain Space, in which the DM is instantiated by

$$\mathbf{D} = \mathbf{T} \tag{3.4}$$

According to this definition, each text t_z in the corpus is considered as a different domain, and the term frequency $\mathbf{t}_{i,z}$ of the term w_i in the text t_z is its domain relevance (i.e. $R(w_i, D_z) = \mathbf{t}_{i,z}$). The rationale of this simple operation can be explained by the lexical coherence assumption. Most of the words expressed in the same texts belong to the same domain. Texts are then "natural" term clusters, and can be exploited to represent the content of other texts by estimating their similarities. In fact, when the DM is defined by Eq. 3.4 and substituted into Eq. 3.1, the ith component of the vector $\mathbf{t'}$ is the dot product $\langle \mathbf{t} \cdot \mathbf{t}_i \rangle$, i.e. the similarity among the two texts t and t' estimated in the Text VSM.

This simple methodology allows us to define a feature representation for texts that takes into account (first-order) relations among terms established by means of their co-occurrences in texts, with the effect of reducing the impact of variability in text similarity estimation, allowing us to compare terms and texts in a common space. On the other hand, this representation is affected by the typical problems of the Term VSM (i.e. high dimensionality and feature sparseness), illustrated in the previous section.

A way to overcome these limitations is to perform a Singular Value Decomposition (SVD) of the term by document matrix $\mathbf{T}$, in order to obtain term and text vectors represented into a lower dimensional space, in which second-order relations among them are taken into account.[4] SVD decomposes the term-by-document matrix $\mathbf{T}$ into three matrixes

[4] In the literature, the term LSA often refers to algorithms that perform the SVD operation before the mapping, even if this operation is just one of the possibilities to implement the general idea behind the definition of the LSA methodology.

$$\mathbf{T} = \mathbf{V}\mathbf{\Sigma}_{\mathbf{k}^*}\mathbf{U}^{\mathrm{T}} \tag{3.5}$$

where $\mathbf{V}^{\mathrm{T}}\mathbf{V} = \mathbf{U}^{\mathrm{T}}\mathbf{U} = I_{k^*}$, $k^* = \min(n,k)$ and $\mathbf{\Sigma}_{\mathbf{k}^*}$ is a diagonal $k^* \times k^*$ matrix such that $\sigma_{r-1,r-1} \geq \sigma_{r,r}$ and $\sigma_{r,r} = 0$ if $r > \mathrm{rank}(\mathbf{T})$. The values $\sigma_{r,r} > 0$ are the non-negative square roots of the n eigenvalues of the matrix $\mathbf{T}\mathbf{T}^{\mathrm{T}}$ and the matrices $\mathbf{V}$ and $\mathbf{U}$ define the orthonormal eigenvectors associated with the eigenvalues of $\mathbf{T}\mathbf{T}^{\mathrm{T}}$ (term-by-term) and $\mathbf{T}^{\mathrm{T}}\mathbf{T}$ (document-by-document), respectively. The components of the Term Vectors in the LSA space can be perceived as the degree of association among terms and clusters of coherent texts. Symmetrically, the components of the Text Vectors in the LSA space are the degree of association between texts and clusters of coherent terms.

The effect of the SVD process is to decompose $\mathbf{T}$ into the product of three matrices, in a way that that the original information contained in it can be exactly reconstructed by multiplying them according to Eq. 3.5. It is also possible to obtain the best approximation $\mathbf{T}_{\mathbf{k}'}$ of rank k' of the matrix $\mathbf{T}$ by substituting the matrix $\mathbf{\Sigma}_{\mathbf{k}'}$ into $\mathbf{\Sigma}_{\mathbf{k}^*}$ in Eq. 3.5. $\mathbf{\Sigma}_{\mathbf{k}'}$ is determined by setting to 0 all the eigenvalues $\sigma_{r,r}$ such that $r > k'$ and $k' \ll \mathrm{rank}(\mathbf{T})$ in the diagonal matrix $\mathbf{\Sigma}_{\mathbf{k}^*}$. The matrix $\mathbf{T}_{\mathbf{k}'} = \mathbf{V}\mathbf{\Sigma}_{\mathbf{k}'}\mathbf{U}^{\mathrm{T}} \simeq \mathbf{T}$ is the best approximation to $\mathbf{T}$ for any unitarily invariant norm, as claimed by the following theorem:

$$\min_{\mathrm{rank}(\mathbf{X})=k'} \|\mathbf{T} - \mathbf{X}\|_2 = \|\mathbf{T} - \mathbf{T}_{\mathbf{k}'}\|_2 = \sigma_{k'+1} \tag{3.6}$$

The parameter k' is the dimensionality of the LSA space and can be fixed in advance.[5] The original matrix can then be reconstructed by adopting fewer number of principal components, allowing us to represent it in a very compact way while preserving most of the information.

Fig. 3.3. Singular Value Decomposition applied to compress a bitmap picture. From the left: the original, and using 5, 20, 80 singular values, respectively

[5] It is not clear how to choose the right dimensionality. Empirically, it has been shown that NLP applications benefit from setting this parameter in the range [50, 400].

This property can be illustrated by applying SVD to a picture represented in a bitmap electronic format, as illustrated by Fig. 3.3, with the effect of compressing the information contained in it. As you can see from the illustration, just a small number of dimensions are required to represent the original information, allowing a good quality reconstruction of the original picture.

Under this setting, we define the domain matrix $\mathbf{D}$ as

$$\mathbf{D} = \mathbf{I}^{\mathrm{N}}\mathbf{V}\sqrt{\mathbf{\Sigma_{k'}}} \tag{3.7}$$

where $\mathbf{I}^{\mathrm{N}}$ is a diagonal matrix such that $\mathbf{i}^{\mathrm{N}}_{\mathbf{i},\mathbf{i}} = \frac{1}{\sqrt{\langle \mathbf{w'}_i, \mathbf{w'}_i \rangle}}$ and $\mathbf{w'}_i$ is the ith row of the matrix $\mathbf{V}\sqrt{\mathbf{\Sigma_{k'}}}$.[6]

Note that Eq. 3.4 differs from Eq. 3.7 just because the term vectors, represented by the row vectors of the left matrix, are expressed in different spaces. In the first case, the Term VSM is used, with the effect of taking into account first-order relations. In the second case, the principal components are identified, allowing a compact and more expressive representation, that takes into account second-order relations. The main improvement of the LSA schema proposed by Eq. 3.7 is that it avoids sparseness, with the effect of reducing noise and capturing variability. In addition, the possibility of keeping the number of domains low, allows us to define a very compact representation for the DM, with the effect of reducing the memory requirements while preserving most of the information. There exist very efficient algorithms to perform the SVD process on sparse matrices, allowing us to perform this operation on large corpora in a very limited time and with reduced memory requirements.

The principal components returned by the SVD process perfectly fit the requirements we ask for a domain set (see Sect. 2.4):

- The domain set is *complete*, because it represents all the terms/documents contained in the corpus.
- The domain set is *balanced* because, by construction, the relevant dimensions explains most of the data in a compact way.
- The domain set is *separated* because, by construction, the principal components are orthogonal.

Throughout the present work, we acquire different DMs from different corpora by performing the SVD processes on the term-by-document matrices representing them.[7] Empirically we observed that augmenting the number of clusters allows us to discover more fine grained domain distinctions.

---

6 The Domain Space is in some sense equivalent to a Latent Semantic Space [22]. The only difference in our formulation is that the vectors representing the terms in the Domain Space are normalized by the matrix $\mathbf{I}^{\mathrm{N}}$, and then rescaled, according to their IDF value, by matrix $\mathbf{I}^{\mathrm{IDF}}$. Note the analogy with the *tf idf* term weighting schema [78], widely adopted in Information Retrieval.

7 To perform the SVD operation we adopted LIBSVDC, an optimized package for sparse matrices that allows us to perform this step in a few minutes even for large corpora. It can be downloaded from `http://tedlab.mit.edu/~dr/SVDLIBC/`.

3.7 The Domain Kernel

In the previous section we described how to build a Domain Model, and in particular a methodology based on a LSA to automatically acquire DMs from a very large corpus. We have shown that DMs provide a very flexible and cheap solution for the problem of modeling domain knowledge. In particular, DMs have been used to define a Domain Space, in which the similarity among terms and texts is estimated.

In this section we introduce the *Domain Kernel*, a similarity function among text and terms that can be exploited by any instance-based supervised learning algorithm in many different NLP applications. This will be the main technique used in the NLP tasks described in the following chapters.

3.7.1 Domain Features in Supervised Learning

Representing linguistic objects by means of relevant semantic features is a basic issue to be solved in order to define any adequate computational model for NLP. When we deal with the problem of defining a solution for a particular task, it is very important to identify *only* the "relevant aspects" to be modeled, avoiding as much as possible irrelevant information. As far as semantics is concerned, the problem of modeling linguistic objects by feature vectors is particularly hard. In principle, the whole picture of human behavior, including its cognitive aspects, can be related to natural language semantics. In practice it has been empirically demonstrated that some well defined feature sets allow successful categorization assessments for a large number of NLP task.

In Sect. 3.2, we claim that the VSM can be profitably used for topic similarity estimation. In Sect. 3.3 we propose the Domain Space as a more expressive model for the same task. We have shown that the Domain Space allows a better similarity estimation, providing non null values among texts and terms even if they do not share any feature and avoiding misleading similarity assessment caused by the lexical ambiguity and feature sparseness. In this section we describe the use of domain-based feature representations for texts and terms in supervised learning, as a way to define a semi-supervised learning schema, in which unsupervised information extracted from unlabeled data can be used inside a supervised framework. In particular DMs can be acquired from unlabeled data, as described in Sect. 3.5, and then used either to extract *domain features* from texts or as a way to perform a better topic similarity estimation among texts.

Many NLP tasks involving semantic analysis of the text can be modeled as classification problems, consisting of assigning category labels to linguistic objects. For example, the Text Categorization (TC) task [80] consists of classifying documents according to a set of semantic classes, domains in our terminology. Similarly, the Term Categorization task [3], is about assigning domain labels to terms in a corpus.

As discussed in Appendix A.2, two main families of supervised learning algorithms can be exploited for this task: feature-based and instance-based classifiers. Feature-based approaches represent the linguistic objects by means of feature vectors. In order to perform a correct discrimination, the feature set should be expressive enough to discriminate the different categories. On the other hand, instance-based approaches rely on the definition of similarity functions among the objects to be classified: in order to allow discrimination the similarity among the objects belonging to the same category is expected to be higher than the similarity among objects belonging to different categories. Both feature-based and instance based approaches require the formulation of task dependent assumptions, in order to take into account the underlying linguistic phenomena involved in the particular task. In addition, we ask any feature representation of objects to be as concise as possible, in order to avoid redundant or irrelevant features.

The domain-based representation for texts and terms can be exploited either by feature-based and by instance-based learning algorithms. In the first case both texts and terms are represented by means of non-sparse domain features, expressing their relevances with respect to a predefined domain set. In the latter case the Domain Space can be used to estimate the similarity among instances, allowing us to define new leaning schemata in which both texts and terms can be represented simultaneously, opening new learning perspectives in NLP. In the next section we will introduce the Domain Kernel, a similarity function among documents that allows us to exploit domain information, acquired from external knowledge sources, inside kernel-based learning algorithms for topic classification. The Domain Kernel performs an explicit dimensionality reduction of the input space, by mapping the vectors from the Text VSM into the Domain Space, improving the generalization capability of the learning algorithm while reducing the amount of training data required. We will provide an extensive empirical evaluation in the following chapters.

The main advantage of adopting domain features is that they allow a dimensionality reduction while they preserve, and sometimes increase, the information that can be expressed by means of a classical VSM representation. This property is crucial from a machine learning perspective. In fact, according to the learning theory [43], the dimensionality of the feature space is related to the Vapnik-Chervonenkis (VC) dimension, that measures the "capacity" of the algorithm (see Appendix A). According to this theory the minimum number of labeled examples m required to guarantee, with probability δ, that the classification error is lower than ϵ, can be determined as follows:

$$m > \frac{1}{\epsilon}\left(4\log_2\frac{2}{\delta} + \mathrm{VC}(H)\log_2\frac{13}{\epsilon}\right) \tag{3.8}$$

where $\mathrm{VC}(H)$ is the Vapnik-Chervonenkis dimension of the hypothesis space H explored by the learning algorithm. In Appendix A we show that the VC dimension of a linear classifier is proportional to the number of features adopted to describe the data. It follows that the higher the number of features, the more labeled data will be required by the learning algorithm to minimize the expected error on the true distribution.

The claims already proposed can be illustrated by the following intuitive argument. DVs for texts and terms are estimated by exploiting the information contained in a DM. In our implementation, we acquired a DM from a SVD process of a term-by-document matrix describing a huge corpus. As illustrated in Sect. 3.6, the effect of SVD is to compress the information contained in the term-by-document matrix describing the corpus by adopting a lower number of dimensions to represent it. The Domain Space allows us to represent the original information contained in the corpus while requiring a lower number of dimensions than the classical VSM, improving the generalization power of the learning algorithm that adopts domain features instead of standard BoWs. In fact, according to Eq. 3.8, the lower the dimensionality of the feature space, the lower the number of training examples required to guarantee the same accuracy.

3.7.2 The Domain Kernel

In this section we describe the *Domain Kernel*, a similarity function among text and terms that can be exploited by any instance-based semi-supervised learning algorithm in many different NLP applications. The Domain Kernel is a Mercer kernel, then it can be adopted by any kernel-based learning algorithm, such as Support Vector Machines (SVMs). SVMs are the state-of-the-art framework for supervised learning. A brief introduction to Kernel Methods for NLP is reported in Appendix A.

The Domain Kernel, denoted by K_{D}, is a kernel function that can be exploited to uniformly estimate the domain similarity among texts and terms while taking into account the external knowledge provided by a DM. The Domain Kernel is implemented by defining an explicit feature mapping that exploits the information contained into the DM to generate DVs for the linguistic objects to which it is applied.

Recalling that a DM is represented by a matrix $\mathbf{D}$, it is possible to define the domain mapping function $\mathcal{D} : \{\mathbf{R}^k \bigcap V\} \rightarrow \mathbf{R}^{k'}$, that maps both texts $\mathbf{t} \in \mathbf{R}^k$ and terms $\mathbf{w} \in \mathbf{R}^n$, into the corresponding DVs $\mathbf{t'} \in \mathbf{R}^{k'}$ and $\mathbf{w'} \in \mathbf{R}^{k'}$ in the same Domain Space. $\mathcal{D}$ is defined by:[8]

$$\mathcal{D}(\mathbf{w}) = \mathbf{w}'_i \;\; ; \text{if } w = w_i \in \mathcal{V}; \qquad (3.9)$$

$$\mathcal{D}(\mathbf{w}) = \frac{\sum_{t \in \mathcal{T}} F(w,t)\mathbf{t}'}{\sqrt{\langle \sum_{t \in \mathcal{T}} F(w,t)\mathbf{t}', \sum_{t \in \mathcal{T}} F(w,t)\mathbf{t}' \rangle}} \;\; ; \text{if } w_i \notin \mathcal{V}; \qquad (3.10)$$

$$\mathcal{D}(\mathbf{t}_j) = \mathbf{t}_j(\mathbf{I}^{\mathrm{IDF}}\mathbf{D}) = \mathbf{t}'_j \qquad (3.11)$$

[8] In [95] a similar schema is adopted to define a Generalized Vector Space Model, of which the Domain Space is a particular instance.

where $\mathbf{w}'_j$ is the DV corresponding to the term w_j,[9] provided by the ith row of $\mathbf{D}$, $F(w,t)$ is the term frequency of w in the text t, $\mathbf{I}^{\text{IDF}}$ is a diagonal matrix representing the Inverse Document Frequency (IDF) of each term (i.e. $\mathbf{I}^{\text{IDF}}_{i,i} = \frac{1}{|\{t \in \mathcal{T} | F(w_i,t)>0\}|}$) and $\mathbf{t}_j$ is the representation of t_j in the Text VSM. Vectors in the Domain Space are called DVs. The similarity among texts and terms is then estimated by evaluating the cosine among the DVs generated in this way.

It is important to remark here that the Domain Kernel is defined for any text and term. In fact, DVs for texts are constructed on the basis of the DVs of the terms they contain, while DVs for terms are either retrieved directly from the DM, or estimated recursively on the basis of the DVs of the texts where they occurs. If required by the application, the novel terms can then be stored directly in the DM, providing a flexible way to create a dynamic and incremental model.

The Domain Kernel is, by construction, a mercer kernel, because it is estimated by means of a dot product in the feature space. Unlike many other kernels, as for example polynomial kernels or string kernels, the mapping function introduced by the Domain Kernel reduces the dimensionality of the feature space instead of increasing it. It follows that the similarity estimation in the feature space will be cheaper than any equivalent estimation in the instance space, unless no sparse feature representations are adopted by the learning algorithm. It then seems unnecessary to define an implicit estimation of the kernel function, as described in [16].[10]

To be fully defined, the Domain Kernel requires a DM $\mathbf{D}$. In principle, $\mathbf{D}$ can be acquired from any corpora by exploiting any term clustering algorithm. Then adopting the Domain Kernel in a supervised learning framework is a way to perform semi-supervised learning, because unlabeled data are provided together with labeled ones.[11]

A more traditional approach to measure topic similarity among text consists of extracting BoW features and to compare them in the VSM. The BoW Kernel, denoted by K_{BoW}, is a particular case of the Domain Kernel, in which $\mathbf{D} = \mathbf{I}$, and $\mathbf{I}$ is the identity matrix. The BoW kernel does not require a DM, so we can consider this setting as "purely" supervised, in which no external knowledge source is provided.

9 Recall that to be a valid DM such vectors should be normalized (i.e. $\langle \mathbf{w}'_i, \mathbf{w}'_i \rangle = 1$).

10 In that work the SVD operation was implicitly performed by the kernel function. In this work we are not interested in such an optimization, because our aim is to acquire the DM from an external corpus, and not from the labeled data themselves.

11 Our experiments confirm the hypothesis that adequate DMs for particular tasks can be better acquired from collections of documents emitted by the same source.

4

Semantic Domains in Text Categorization

In the previous chapter we have shown that DMs provide a very flexible and cheap solution for the problem of modeling domain knowledge. In particular, DMs have been used to define a Domain Space, in which the similarity among terms and texts is estimated.

We will show how to exploit DMs inside a supervised machine learning framework, in order to provide "external" knowledge to supervised NLP systems, which can be profitably used for topic similarity estimation. In particular we exploit a Domain Kernel (defined in Sect. 3.7), a similarity function among terms and texts that can be used by any kernel-based learning algorithm, with the effect of avoiding the problems of lexical variability and ambiguity.

In this chapter we show the advantages of domain-based feature representation in supervised learning, approaching the problem of Text Categorization. In particular we will evaluate the Domain Kernel in two tasks: Text Categorization (see Sect. 4.1) and Intensional Learning (see Sect. 4.2).

4.1 Domain Kernels for Text Categorization

In this section we evaluate the Domain Kernel in a Text Categorization task. Text Categorization deals with the problem of assigning a set of category labels to documents. Categories are usually defined according to a variety of topics (e.g. SPORT vs. POLITICS) and a set of hand tagged examples is collected to train a supervised classifier.

As illustrated in Sect. 3.2, the task to assign semantic classes to text is intimately related to the problem of topic similarity estimation. In that section, it has been claimed that BoW features are able to represent most of the relevant text descriptions required to correctly perform this task. This claim is supported by the success of the present Text Categorization technology: state-of-the-art supervised approaches to Text Categorization represent texts by means of BoWs. In Sect. 3.7.1 it has been also remarked that a simple BoW approach to text indexing is not adequate to deal with the problems of

A. Gliozzo and C. Strapparava, *Semantic Domains in Computational Linguistics*,
DOI: 10.1007/978-3-540-68158-8_4, © Springer-Verlag Berlin Heidelberg 2009

ambiguity and variability. Both problems are particularly relevant in the Text Categorization settings, in which the number of labeled training documents is often too small to guarantee a small prediction error (see Sect. 3.7.1). For example, the category models inferred by feature-based linear classifiers for Text Categorization (e.g. Perceptron [19], Rocchio [67], ADA-Boost [80]) are represented by means of weighted lists of discriminative terms. Ambiguous terms will be reflected in noisy profiles, while variability will lead to incompleteness in the learned category profiles (e.g. if only the term money is included in the profile of the category ECONOMY, a text containing the term cash would not be correctly categorized).

The Domain Kernel, introduced in Sect. 3.7, is an attempt to overcome such limitations. In our implementation, the Domain Kernel performs an explicit feature mapping from the Text VSM into the Domain Space, in which the similarity among texts is estimated by taking into account the information provided by a DM, acquired from unlabeled data. As we will show in the next subsection, adopting the Domain Kernel in a SVM classification framework is a viable strategy to design a semi-supervised learning schema for Text Categorization. In Subsect. 4.1.2 we evaluate the Domain Kernel against a state-of-the-art BoW kernel for Text Categorization [42], reporting substantial improvements in recall, while preserving the precision of the algorithm.

4.1.1 Semi-supervised Learning in Text Categorization

Even if, in principle, supervised approaches reach the best performance in many NLP tasks, in practice it is not always easy to apply them to concrete applicative settings. In fact, supervised systems for Text Categorization need large amounts of hand tagged texts. The applicability of supervised Text Categorization systems is then restricted to application scenarios in which it is possible to easily provide large amounts of manually categorized documents to train the system, as for example for big companies. This solution is often unpractical, when not infeasible. An example is the task of categorizing personal documents, in which the category set is frequently modified according to the user's interests: new categories are often introduced and, possibly, the available labeled training for them is very limited.

In the NLP literature the problem of providing large amounts of manually annotated data is known as the knowledge acquisition bottleneck. Current research in supervised approaches to NLP often deals with defining methodologies and algorithms to reduce the amount of human effort required for collecting labeled examples.

A promising direction to solve this problem is to provide unlabeled data together with labeled texts to help supervision. In the machine learning literature this learning schema has been called *semi-supervised learning*.

To our knowledge, the first attempt to apply the semi-supervised learning schema to Text Categorization has been reported in [8]. Their co-training algorithm was able to reduce significantly the error rate, if compared to a strictly supervised classifier.

[70] adopted an Expectation Maximization schema to deal with the same problem, evaluating extensively this approach on several data sets. They compared their algorithm with a standard probabilistic approach to Text Categorization, reporting a substantial improvement in the learning curve.

A similar evaluation is also reported in [41], where a transduptive SVM is compared to a state-of-the-art Text Categorization classifier based on SVM. The semi-supervised approach obtained better results than the standard with few learning data, while at full learning results seem to converge.

[5] adopted a SVM classifier in which texts have been represented by their associations to a set of distributional word clusters. Even if this approach is very similar to ours, it is not a semi-supervised learning schema, because the authors did not exploit any additional unlabeled data to induce word clusters.

In [99] background knowledge (i.e. the unlabeled data) is exploited together with labeled data to estimate document similarity in a Latent Semantic Space [22]. Their approach differs from the one proposed in this section because a different categorization algorithm has been adopted. The authors compared their algorithm with an Expectation Maximization schema [70] on the same data set, reporting better results only with very few labeled data, while Expectation Maximization performs better with more training.

In this section, we show that the Domain Kernel can be used to implement a semi-supervised learning schema for Text Categorization. Our proposal consists on defining a Domain Kernel that exploits DMs acquired from unlabeled text collections, and to use them inside a SVM supervised classification framework for Text Categorization [42].

4.1.2 Evaluation

We compared the performance of both the Domain and the BoW Kernels, respectively denoted by K_{D} and K_{BoW}, on two standard Text Categorization benchmarks. Here below we describe the evaluation tasks, the preprocessing steps and some algorithmic details of the Text Categorization systems adopted. Finally we analyzed the learning curves of K_{D} and K_{BoW}, reporting a comparison with the state-of-the-art in those tasks. The results reported below have been also presented in [31].

Text Categorization Tasks

For the Text Categorization experiments, we selected two evaluation benchmarks typically used in the literature [80]: the *20-Newsgroups* and the *Reuters* corpora. In both the data sets we tagged the texts for PoS and we considered only nouns, verbs, adjectives, and adverbs, representing them by vectors containing the frequencies of each disambiguated lemma. The only feature selection step we performed was to remove all the closed-class words from the document index.

20-Newsgroups

The *20-Newsgroups* data set[1] is a collection of approximately 20,000 newsgroup documents, partitioned (nearly) evenly across 20 different newsgroups. This collection has become a popular data set for experiments in text applications of machine learning techniques, such as Text Categorization and Text Clustering. Some of the newsgroups are very closely related to each other (e.g. COMP.SYS.IBM.PC.HARDWARE and COMP.SYS.MAC.HARDWARE), while others are highly unrelated (e.g. MISC.FORSALE and SOC.RELIGION.CHRISTIAN). We removed cross-posts (duplicates), newsgroup-identifying headers (i.e. Xref, Newsgroups, Path, Followup-To, Date), and empty documents from the original corpus, so to obtain 18,941 documents. Then we randomly divided it into training (80%) and test (20%) sets, containing respectively 15,153 and 3788 documents.

Reuters

We used the *Reuters-21578* collection,[2] and we split it into training and test partitions according to the standard *ModAptè* split. It includes 12,902 documents for 90 categories, with a fixed splitting between training and test data. We conducted our experiments by considering only the 10 most frequent categories, i.e. EARN, ACQUISITION, MONEY-FX, GRAIN, CRUDE, TRADE, INTEREST, SHIP, WHEAT and CORN, and we included in our data set all the non empty documents labeled with at least one of those categories. Thus the final data set includes 9295 document, out of which 6680 are included in the training partition, and 2615 are in the test set.

Implementation Details

As a supervised learning device, we used the SVM implementation described in [40]. The Domain Kernel performs an explicit feature mapping, as described in Sect. 3.7. All the experiments have been performed on the standard parameter settings. We acquired a different DM for each benchmark by performing the SVD processes on the term-by-document matrices representing the whole training partitions, and we considered only the first 400 domains (i.e. $k' = 400$).

As far as the *Reuters* task is concerned, the Text Categorization problem has been approached as a set of binary filtering problems, allowing the system to provide more than one category label to each document. For the *20-Newsgroups* task, we implemented a one-versus-all classification schema, in order to assign a single category to each news.

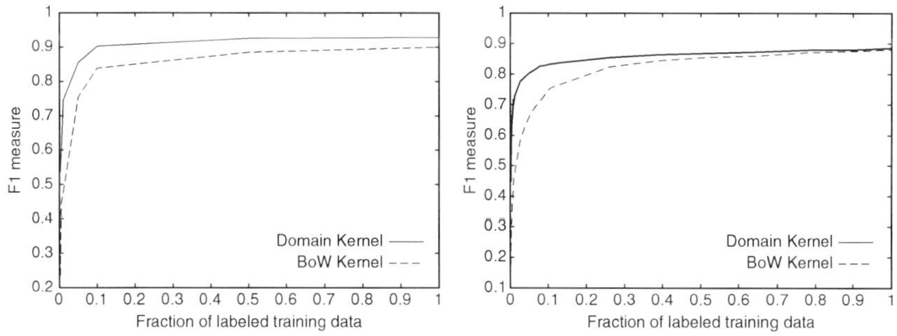

Fig. 4.1. Micro-F1 learning curves for *Reuters* (left) and *20-Newsgroups* (right)

Domain Kernel vs. Bag-of-Words Kernel

Figure 4.1 reports the learning curves for both K_{D} and K_{BoW}, evaluated on the *Reuters* (left) and the *20-Newgroups* (right) tasks. Results clearly show that K_{D} always outperforms K_{BoW}, especially when very limited amounts of labeled data are provided for learning.

Table 4.1. Micro-F1 with full learning

F1	*Domain Kernel*	*Bow Kernel*
Reuters	**0.928**	0.900
20-Newsgroups	**0.886**	0.880

Table 4.1 compares the performances of the two kernels at full learning. K_{D} achieves a better micro-F1 than K_{BoW} in both tasks. The improvement is particularly significant in the *Reuters* task (+ 2.8 %).

Table 4.2 shows the number of labeled examples required by K_{D} and K_{BoW} to achieve the same micro-F1 in the *Reuters* task. K_{D} requires only 146 examples to obtain a micro-F1 of 0.84, while K_{BoW} requires 1380 examples to achieve the same performance. In the same task, K_{D} surpasses the performance of K_{BoW} at full learning using only 10% of the labeled data. The last column of the table shows clearly that K_{D} requires 90% less labeled data than K_{BoW} to achieve the same performances.

[1] Available at `http://www.ai.mit.edu/people/jrennie/20Newsgroups/`.

[2] Available at `http://kdd.ics.uci.edu/databases/reuters21578/-reuters21578.html`.

Table 4.2. Number of training examples needed by K_{D} and K_{BoW} to reach the same micro-F1 on the *Reuters* task

F1	*Domain Kernel*	*Bow Kernel*	*Ratio*
.54	**14**	267	5%
.84	**146**	1380	10%
.90	**668**	6680	10%

Table 4.3. Number of training examples needed by K_{D} and K_{BoW} to reach the same micro-F1 on the *20-Newsgroups* task

F1	*Domain Kernel*	*Bow Kernel*	*Ratio*
.50	**30**	500	6%
.70	**98**	1182	8%
.85	**2272**	7879	29%

Similar behavior is reported in Table 4.3 for the *20-Newsgroups* task. It is important to notice that the number of labeled documents is higher in this corpus than in the previous one. The benefits of using DMs are then less evident at full learning, even if they are significant when very few labeled data are provided.

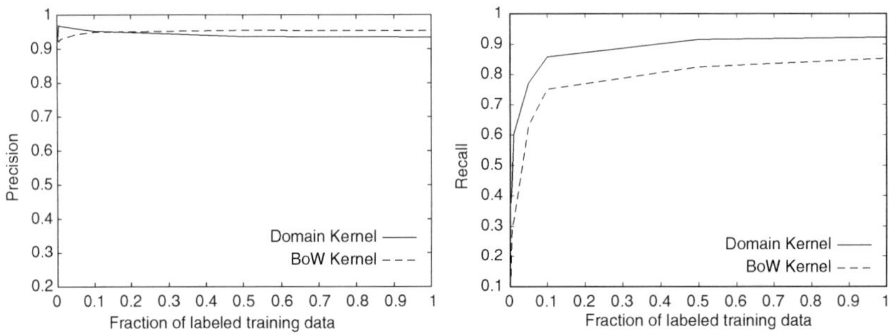

Fig. 4.2. Precision (left) and recall (right) learning curves for *Reuters*

Figure 4.2 reports a more detailed analysis by comparing the micro-precision (left) and micro-recall (right) learning curves of both kernels in the

Reuters task.[3] It is clear from the graphs that the main contribution of K_D is about increasing recall, while precision is similar in both cases.[4] This last result confirms our hypothesis that the information provided by the DMs allows the system to generalize in a more effective way over the training examples, allowing to estimate the similarity among texts even if they have just few words in common.

Comparison to the State-of-the-Art

A comparative evaluation among semi supervised TC algorithms is quite difficult, because the used data sets, the preprocessing steps and the splitting partitions adopted sensibly affect the final results. Anyway, we reported the best F1 measure on the *Reuters* corpus: to our knowledge, the state-of-the-art on the 10 top most frequent categories of the ModApte split at full learning is F1 0.920 [5], while we obtained 0.928. It is important to notice here that this result has been obtained thanks to the improvements of the Domain Kernel. In addition, on the *20-Newsgroups* task, our method requires about 100 documents (i.e. five documents per category) to achieve 0.70 F1, while both the Expectation Maximization algorithm presented by [70] and the method based on Latent Semantic Indexing described in [99] requires more than 400 to achieve the same performance.

4.1.3 Discussion

In this section we described a semi-supervised approach to Text Categorization that relies on the exploitation of the Domain Kernel, and we evaluated it in two standard Text Categorization benchmarks. A comparison between the Domain and the BOW Kernels shows that DM, acquired from unlabeled data, allows us to uniformly improve the similarity estimation among documents, with the basic effect of increasing the recall while preserving the precision of the algorithm. This effect is particularly evident when just small amounts of labeled data are provided for learning. A comparison with the state-of-the-art shows that the Domain Kernel achieves the highest result ever reported for the *Reuters* task with full learning, even if the same result is not achieved for the *20-Newsgroups*. The Domain Kernel can be easily implemented, by simply providing the learning algorithm of large amounts of unlabeled data, that can be easily collected, and represents a technologically viable solution for the Text Categorization task, that can be easily applied to the user modeling setting. In fact the Domain Kernel is able to achieve good results even if

[3] For the 20-newsgroups task both micro-precision and micro-recall are equal to micro-F1 because a single category label has been assigned to every instance.

[4] It is worth noting that K_D gets a F1 measure of 0.54 (Precision/Recall of 0.93/0.38) using just 14 training examples, suggesting that it can be profitably exploited for a bootstrapping process.

less then ten examples per category are provided, allowing us to easily define category profiles by means of a limited manual annotation.

4.2 Intensional Learning

In this section we investigate a fundamental property of the Domain Space: the duality between texts and terms (see Sect. 3.3). In the Domain Space both terms and texts are represented homogeneously by means of their DVs, which can be induced from their VSM representation. This property is of great interest to define an Intensional Learning (IL) schema for Text Categorization, in which each category is described by providing a set of relevant terms, called an *Intensional Description* (ID), and a training corpus of unlabeled texts is provided. The definition of the Domain Kernel fits the IL settings perfectly. In fact, unlabeled texts can be used to acquire DMs, and the Domain Kernel can be exploited to compare the similarity among seeds and the unlabeled texts, to define a preliminary association among terms and texts.

In this section we propose the use of the Domain Kernel as a component of a generalized bootstrapping algorithm in which categories are described by relevant seed features. In addition we introduce an unsupervised algorithm, named the Gaussian Mixture algorithm, to define a categorization criterion that maps the similarity scores provided by the Domain Kernel into probabilities. Then a supervised algorithm for Text Categorization based on SVM has been trained on the (estimated) positive examples for each class.

The bootstrapping algorithm defined in this way has been evaluated on two Text Categorization tasks and obtained state-of-the-art performance using only the category names as initial seeds. As shown in our experiments, incorporating these steps consistently improved the accuracy of the initial categorization step, which in turn yielded a better final classifier thanks to the more accurate training set. Most importantly, we obtained comparable or better performance than previous IL methods using *only* the category names as the seed features; other IL methods required collecting a larger number of seed terms, which turns out to be a somewhat tricky task. In the rest of this section we will mainly refer to the previous work reported in [33]

4.2.1 Intensional Learning for Text Categorization

As fully discussed in Appendix A.1, supervised classification is the task of assigning category labels, taken from a predefined set of categories, to instances in a data set. Within the classical supervised learning paradigm, the task is approached by providing a learning algorithm with a training set of manually labeled examples. In practice it is not always easy to apply this schema to NLP tasks. As discussed in Subsect. 4.1.1, supervised systems for Text Categorization require a large amount of hand labeled texts, while in many applicative cases it is quite difficult to collect the required amounts of hand labeled data. Unlabeled text collections, on the other hand, are in general easily available. In Sect. 4.1 we proposed semi-supervised learning as a viable strategy to minimize the amount of supervision required. In this section we propose IL as an alternative approach to achieve the same goal.

In the IL settings, the necessary supervision is provided by means of sets of "seeds" of intuitively relevant features instead of labeled texts. Adopting terminology from computability theory, we refer to the standard example-based supervision mode as *Extensional Learning*, as classes are being specified by means of examples of their elements (their *extension*). Feature-based supervision is referred to as IL, as features may often be perceived as describing the *intension* of a category, such as providing the name or prominent key terms for a category in Text Categorization.[5]

The IL approach dates from classical rule-based classification methods, where the user is expected to specify exact classification rules that operate in the feature space. Within the machine learning paradigm, IL has been incorporated as a technique for bootstrapping an extensional learning algorithm, as in [97, 13, 54]. In this way, the user does not need to specify exact classification rules (and feature weights), but rather performs a somewhat simpler task of specifying few typical seed features for the category. Given the list of seed features, the bootstrapping scheme consists of (i) preliminary unsupervised categorization of the unlabeled data set based on the seed features, and (ii) training an (extensional) supervised classifier using the automatic classification labels of step (i) for training (the second step is possibly reiterated, such as by an Expectation-Maximization schema). The core part of IL bootstrapping is step (i), i.e. the initial unsupervised classification of the unlabeled data set. This step was often approached by relatively simple methods, which are doomed to obtain mediocre quality. Even so, it is hoped that the second step of supervised training would be robust enough to the noise in the initial training set.

As discussed in Sect. 4.1, the Text Categorization task is to assign category labels to documents. In the IL setting, a category C_i is described by providing an ID (i.e. a set of relevant features: $id_{c_i} \subseteq \mathcal{V}$, where $\mathcal{V}$ is the vocabulary). In addition a training corpus $\mathcal{T} = \{t_1, t_2, \ldots t_n\}$ of *unlabeled* texts is provided. Evaluation is performed on a separate test corpus of labeled documents, to which standard evaluation metrics can be applied.

The approach of categorizing texts based on lists of keywords has been attempted rather rarely in the literature [61, 46, 54, 47]. Several names have been proposed for it – such as *Text Categorization by bootstrapping with keywords*, *unsupervised Text Categorization*, *Text Categorization by labeling words*

[5] It is important to distinguish here between feature-based categorization and feature-based supervision. The former, discussed in Appendix A, consists of describing the instances by means of relevant features, in opposition to instance-based learning; the latter is a way to provide the required supervision to the system, in opposition to instance-based supervision, in which labeled data are provided to describe categories.

– where the proposed methods fall (mostly) within the IL settings described here.[6] It is possible to recognize a common structure of these works, based on a typical bootstrap schema [97, 13]:

Step 1: *Initial unsupervised categorization.* This step was approached by applying some similarity criterion between the initial category seed and each unlabeled document. Similarity may be determined as a binary criterion, considering each seed keyword as a classification rule [61], or by applying a similarity measure in the VSM. The result of this step is an initial categorization of (a subset of) the unlabeled documents. In [47] term similarity techniques were exploited to expand the set of seed keywords, in order to improve the quality of the initial categorization.

Step 2: *Train a supervised classifier on the initially categorized set.* The output of Step 1 is exploited to train an (extensional) supervised classifier. Different learning algorithms have been tested, including SVM, Naive Bayes, Nearest Neighbors, and Rocchio. Some works [61, 54] performed an additional Expectation Maximization algorithm over the training data, but reported rather small incremental improvements that do not seem to justify the additional effort.

[61] reported categorization results close to human agreement on the same task. [54] and [47] contrasted their word-based Text Categorization algorithm with the performance of an extensional supervised algorithm, achieving comparable results, while in general somewhat lower. It should be noted that it has been more difficult to define a common evaluation framework for comparing IL algorithms for Text Categorization, due to the subjective selection of seed IDs and to the lack of common IL test sets (see Subsect. 4.2.3).

4.2.2 Domain Models and the Gaussian Mixture Algorithm for Intensional Learning

In this subsection we show how the core Step 1 of the IL scheme – the initial categorization – can be boosted by two unsupervised techniques. These techniques fit the IL setting and address its major constraints. The first is exploiting the Domain Kernel to define a generalized similarity metric between category seeds (IDs) and instances. Applying such an unsupervised similarity enables us to enhance the amount of information that is exploited from each seed feature, aiming to reduce the number of needed seeds. The second technique applies the unsupervised *Gaussian Mixture* (GM) algorithm, which maps in a principled way similarity scores to classification probability values. This step enables us to obtain a uniform scale of classification scores across all

[6] The major exception is the work in [47], which largely follows the IL scheme but then makes use of labeled data to perform a chi-square based feature selection before starting the bootstrap process. This clearly falls outside the IL setting, making their results incomparable to other IL methods.

categories, which is typically obtained only through calibration over labeled examples in extensional learning.

Duality in the Domain Space

As explained above, Step 1 of the IL scheme assesses a degree of "match" between the seed terms and a classified document. It is possible first to follow the intuitively appealing and principled approach of [54], in which IDs (category seeds) and instances are represented by vectors in the VSM, and similarity is measured by the cosine function. To perform this operation we can adopt the BoW kernel (i.e. K_{BoW}), defined in Sect. 3.7.

However, the VSM representation for seeds and instances is severely affected by feature sparseness in the IL settings. In general, IDs are composed by short lists of features, possibly just a single feature. Due to data sparseness, most instances do not contain any feature in common with any category ID, which makes the seeds irrelevant for many of them. Furthermore, applying direct matching only for a few seed terms is often too crude, as it ignores the identity of the other terms in the document. The above problems may be reduced by considering some form of similarity in the feature space, as it enables us to compare additional document terms with the original seeds. As mentioned in Subsect. 4.2.1, [47] explicitly expanded the original category IDs with more terms, using a concrete query expansion scheme.

As described throughout this chapter, the Domain Kernel allows us to estimate the similarity among terms and texts in the Domain Space, in which a better generalization is allowed by taking into account second order relations. In the Domain Space both coherent terms (i.e. terms that often co-occur in the same texts) and coherent texts (i.e. texts that share coherent terms) are represented by similar vectors in the reduced dimensionality space. As a result, a text would be considered similar to a category ID if the seed terms and the text terms tend to co-occur overall in the given corpus. The Domain Kernel $K_{\mathrm{D}}(c_i, t_j)$ can then be exploited to estimate the similarity among the category descriptions c_i and texts t_j. In Subsect. 4.2.3 we will show that using such a non-sparse representation allows us to drastically reduce the number of seeds required to define each category, while improving significantly the recall of the initial categorization step.

The Gaussian Mixture Algorithm

Once having a similarity function between category IDs and instances, a simple strategy is to base the classification decision (of Step 1) directly on the obtained similarity values (as in [54], for example). Typically, IL works adopt in Step 1 a single-label classification approach, and classify each instance (document) to only one category. The chosen category is the one whose ID is most similar to the classified instance amongst all categories, which does not require any threshold tuning over labeled examples. The subsequent training in Step

2 yields a standard Extensional Learning classifier, which can then be used to assign multiple categories to a document.

Using directly the output of the similarity function for classification is problematic, because the obtained scales of similarity values vary substantially across different categories. The variability in similarity value ranges is caused by variations in the number of seed terms per category and the levels of their generality and ambiguity. As a consequence, choosing the class with the highest absolute similarity value to the instance often leads to selecting a category whose similarity values tend to be generally higher, while another category could have been more similar to the classified instance if normalized similarity values were used.

As a solution we propose using an algorithm based on unsupervised estimation of GMs, which differentiates relevant and non-relevant category information using statistics from unlabeled instances. We recall that mixture models have been widely used in pattern recognition and statistics to approximate probability distributions. In particular, a well-known non-parametric method for density estimation is the so-called Gaussian Mixture Model [82], which approximates an unknown density with a mixture of Gaussian functions. Under mild regularity conditions of the unknown density function, it can be shown that mixtures of Gaussians converge, in a statistical sense, to *any* distribution.

More formally, let $t_i \in T$ be an object and let $id_{c_i} \subset V$ be the ID of category C_i; let $K(id_{c_i}, t_j) \in \mathbf{R}$ be a similarity function among instances and IDs, with the only expectation that it monotonically increases according to the "closeness" of id_{c_i} and t_j.[7] For each category C_i, GM induces a mapping from the similarity scores between its ID and any instance t_j, $K(id_{c_i}, t_j)$, into the probability of C_i given the text t_j, $P(C_i|t_j)$. To achieve this goal GM performs the following operations: (i) it computes the set $\mathcal{S}_i = \{K(id_{c_i}, t_j)|t_j \in T\}$ of the similarity scores between the ID id_{c_i} of the category C_i and all the instances t_j in the unlabeled training set T; (ii) it induces from the empirical distribution of values in $\mathcal{S}_i$ a GM distribution which is composed of two "hypothetic" distributions $\mathcal{C}_i$ and $\overline{\mathcal{C}_i}$, which are assumed to describe respectively the distributions of similarity scores for positive and negative examples; and (iii) it estimates the conditional probability $P(C_i|K(id_{c_i}, t_j))$ by applying the Bayes theorem on the distributions $\mathcal{C}_i$ and $\overline{\mathcal{C}}_i$. These steps are explained in more detail below.

The core idea of the algorithm is in step (ii). Since we do not have labeled training examples we can only obtain the set $\mathcal{S}_i$ which includes the similarity scores for all examples together, both positive and negative. We assume, however, that similarity scores that correspond to positive examples are drawn from one distribution, $P(K(id_{c_i}, t_j)|C_i)$, while the similarity scores

[7] Of course, any kernel function can be exploited simply as a similarity function. In the case of the GM algorithm, it is not asked for K to be a Mercer kernel, because this function is not used for supervised learning in a dual space, see Appendix A.

that correspond to negative examples are drawn from another distribution, $P(K(id_{c_i}, t_j)|\overline{C_i})$. The observed distribution of similarity values in $\mathcal{S}_i$ is thus assumed to be a mixture of the above two distributions, which are recovered by the GM estimation.

Figure 4.3 illustrates the mapping induced by GM from the empirical mixture distribution: dotted lines describe the PDFs estimated by GM for $\mathcal{C}$, $\overline{\mathcal{C}}$. Their mixture approximates the empirical distribution $\mathcal{S}_c$. The continuous line is the mapping of the algorithm from similarity scores between instances and IDs (x-axis) to the probability of the instance to belong to the category (y-axis).

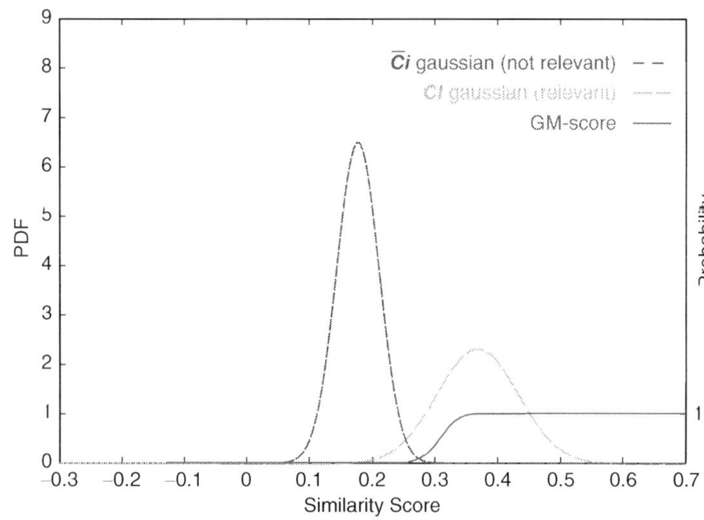

Fig. 4.3. Mapping induced by GM for the category REC.MOTORCYCLES in the *20-Newsgroups* data set

The probabilistic mapping estimated in step (iii) for a category C_i given an instance t_j is computed by applying the Bayes rule:

$$P(C_i|t_j) = P(C_i|K(id_{c_i}, t_j)) \tag{4.1}$$
$$= \frac{P(K(id_{c_i}, t_j)|C_i)P(C_i)}{P(K(id_{c_i}, t_j)|C_i)P(C_i) + P(K(C_i, t_j)|\overline{C_i})P(\overline{C_i})}$$

where $P(K(id_{c_i}, t_j)|C_i)$ is the value of the PDF of $\mathcal{C}_i$ at the point $K(id_{c_i}, t_j)$, $P(K(id_{c_i}, t_j)|\overline{C_i})$ is the value of the PDF of $\overline{\mathcal{C}_i}$ at the same point, $P(C_i)$ is the area of the distribution $\mathcal{C}_i$ and $P(\overline{C_i})$ is the area of the distribution $\overline{\mathcal{C}_i}$. The mean and variance parameters of the two distributions $\mathcal{C}_i$ and $\overline{\mathcal{C}_i}$, used to evaluate Eq. 4.1, are estimated by the rather simple application of the

Expectation Maximization (EM) algorithm for Gaussian Mixtures, as summarized in [32]. Finally, following the single-labeled categorization setting of Step 1 in the IL schema, the most likely category is assigned to each instance, that is, $\text{argmax}_{C_i} P(C_i|t_j)$.

4.2.3 Evaluation

In this section we extensively evaluate our bootstrapping algorithm for IL, showing that the Domain Kernel is superior to the BoW Kernel to perform Step 1, leading the overall algorithm to achieve better results. We also show the benefits of adopting the GM algorithm as a categorization criterion.

It will be demonstrated that the Domain Kernel allows us to use just the category name as a category ID for each class, in contrast to the classical VSM representation, that requires many more features to obtain lower results.

Intensional Text Categorization Data Sets

Even though some typical data sets have been used in the Text Categorization literature [80], the data sets used for IL learning were not standard. Often there is not sufficient clarity regarding details such as the exact version of the corpus used and the training/test splitting. Furthermore, the choice of categories was often not standard: [47] omitted four categories from the *20-Newsgroup* data set, while [54] evaluated their method on four separate subsets of the *20-Newsgroups*, each containing only 4-5 categories. Such issues make it rather difficult to thoroughly compare different techniques, yet we have conducted several comparisons. In the remainder of this subsection we clearly state the corpora used in our experiments and the preprocessing steps performed on them.

20-Newsgroups

The *20-Newsgroups* data set is a collection of newsgroup documents, partitioned (nearly) evenly across 20 different newsgroups (see Subsect. 4.1.2). As suggested in the data set web site,[8] we used the "bydate" version: the corpus (18,941 documents) is sorted by date and divided in advance into a training (60%) set and a chronologically following test set (40%) (so there is no randomness in train/test set selection); it does not include cross-posts (duplicates), and (more importantly) does not include non-textual newsgroup-identifying headers which often help classification (Xref, Newsgroups, Path, Followup-To, Date).

We will first report results using *initial seeds* for the category ID's, which were selected using only the words in the category names, with some trivial transformations (i.e. {cryptography#n} for the category SCI.CRYPT, {x-windows#n} for the category COMP.WINDOWS.X). We also tried to avoid "overlapping" seeds, i.e. for the categories REC.SPORT.BASEBALL and REC.SPORT.HOCKEY

[8] The collection is available at `www.ai.mit.edu/people/jrennie/20Newsgroups`.

the seeds are only {baseball#n} and {hockey#n} respectively and not {sport#n, baseball#n} and {sport#n, hockey#n}.[9]

Reuters-10

We used the top 10 categories (*Reuters-10*) in the *Reuters-21578* collection Aptè split, adopting the same settings as described in Subsect. 4.1.2. The initial seeds are only the words appearing in the category names.

Pre-processing

In both data sets we tagged the texts for PoS and represented the documents by the frequency of each PoS-tagged lemma, considering only nouns, verbs, adjectives, and adverbs. We induce the DMs from the training part[10] and consider the first 400 dimensions.

The Impact of Domain Models and Gaussian Mixtures

In this section we evaluate the incremental impact of the similarity estimation provided by the Domain Kernel and the GM algorithm on IL performance. When avoiding both techniques the algorithm uses the simple K_{BoW} kernel over the original feature space, which can be considered as a baseline (similar to the method of [54]). We report first results using only the names of the categories as initial seeds.

Table 4.4 displays the F1 measure for the *20-Newsgroups* and *Reuters-10* data sets, contrasting both the results obtained by the Domain Kernel to those obtained by the BoW Kernel and the performances of our algorithm with and without GM. The performance figures show the incremental benefit of both the Domain Kernel and GM. In particular, when starting with just initial seeds and not exploiting the Domain Space to estimate similarity among IDs and texts, the performance is heavily penalized.

As mentioned above, the bootstrapping step of the IL algorithm (Step 2) exploits the initially classified instances to train a supervised Text Categorization classifier based on SVM. It is worthwhile noting that the increment

[9] One could propose as a guideline for seed selection those seeds that maximize their distances in the LSI vector space model. On this perspective the LSI vectors built from {sport#n, baseball#n} and {sport#n, hockey#n} are closer than the vectors that represent {baseball#n} and {hockey#n}. It may be noticed that this is a reason for the slight initial performance decrease in the learning curve in Fig. 4.4 below.

[10] From a machine learning point of view, we could run the acquisition process on the full corpus (i.e. training and test), the SVD being a completely unsupervised technique (i.e. it does not take into account the data annotation). However, from an applicative point of view it is much more sensible to have the DMs built on the training part only. If we run this process on the full corpus, the performance figures should increase by about four points.

Table 4.4. Impact of the Domain Kernel and GM in the IL performances

			Reuters	*20-Newsgroups*
	K	*GM*	*F1*	*F1*
	K_{BoW}	no	0.38	0.25
+ *bootstrap*			0.42	0.28
	K_{BoW}	yes	0.41	0.30
+ *bootstrap*			0.46	0.34
	K_D	no	0.46	0.50
+ *bootstrap*			**0.47**	**0.53**
	K_D	yes	0.58	0.60
+ *bootstrap*			**0.74**	**0.65**

of performance after bootstrapping is generally higher when GM and the Domain Kernel are used, thanks to the higher quality of the initial categorization which was used for training.

Learning Curves for the Number of Seeds

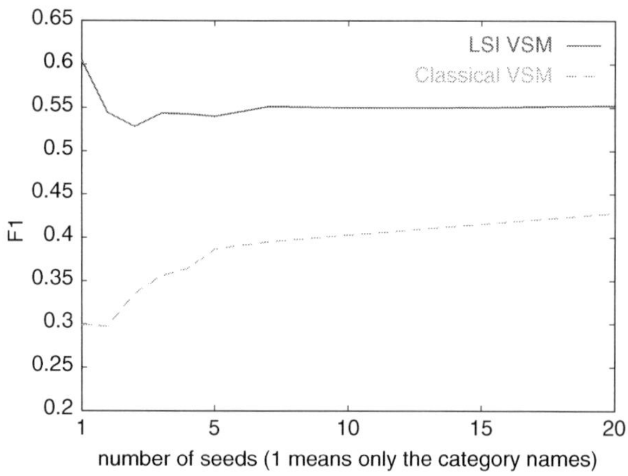

Fig. 4.4. Learning curves on initial seeds: Domain vs. BoW Kernel

This experiment evaluates accuracy change as a function of the number of initial seeds. The experiment was performed for the *20-Newsgroups* corpus using both the Domain and the BoW Kernels. Additional seeds, beyond the category names, were identified by two lexicographers. For each category, the lexicographers were provided with a list of 100 seeds obtained by retrieving the more similar terms to the category name in the Domain Space. From these lists the lexicographers selected the words that were judged as significantly related to the respective category, picking a mean of 40 seeds per category.

As seen in Fig. 4.4, the learning curve using the Domain Kernel dramatically outperforms the one using the BoW kernel. As can be expected, when using the Text VSM (no generalization) the curve improves quickly with a few more terms. More surprisingly, the Domain Kernel is characterized by an opposite trend: the best performance is obtained using the minimal initial seeds of the category names, while adding more seeds degrades performance. This might suggest that category names tend to be highly indicative for the intensional meaning of the category, and therefore adding more terms introduces additional noise. Further research is needed to find out whether other methods for selecting additional seed terms might yield incremental improvements. The current results, though, emphasize the benefit of utilizing the Domain Kernel and GM. These techniques obtain state-of-the-art performance (see comparisons in Subsect. 4.2.3) using only the category names as seeds, allowing us to skip the quite tricky phase of collecting manually a larger number of seeds.

Extensional vs. Intensional Learning

A major point of comparison between IL and Extensional Learning is the amount of supervision effort required to obtain a certain level of performance. To this end we trained an (extensional) supervised classifier based on SVM, and draw its learning curves as a function of percentage of the training set size (Fig. 4.5). In the case of *20-Newsgroups*, to achieve the 65% F1 performance of IL the supervised settings requires about 3200 documents (about 160 texts per category), while our IL method requires only the category name. *Reuters-10* is an easier corpus, therefore Extensional Learning achieves rather rapidly a high performance. But even here using just the category name is equal on average to labeling 70 documents per-category (700 in total).

These results suggest that IL may provide an appealing cost-effective alternative in practical settings when sub-optimal accuracy suffices, or when it is too costly or impractical to obtain sufficient amounts of labeled training sets. It should also be stressed that when using the complete labeled training corpus state-of-the-art Extensional Learning outperforms our best IL performance. This result deviates from the flavor of previous IL literature, which reported almost comparable performance relative to Extensional Learning. As mentioned earlier, the method of [47] (as we understand it) utilizes labeled examples for feature selection, and therefore cannot be compared with our strict IL setting. As for the results in [54], we conjecture that their comparable performance for IL and Extensional Learning may not be sufficiently general, for several reasons: the easier classification task (four subsets of *20-Newsgroups* of 4-5 categories each); the use of the usually weaker Naive-Bayes as the Extensional Learning device; the use of clustering as an aid for selecting the seed terms from the *20-Newsgroup* subsets, which might not scale up well when applied to a large number of categories of different size.

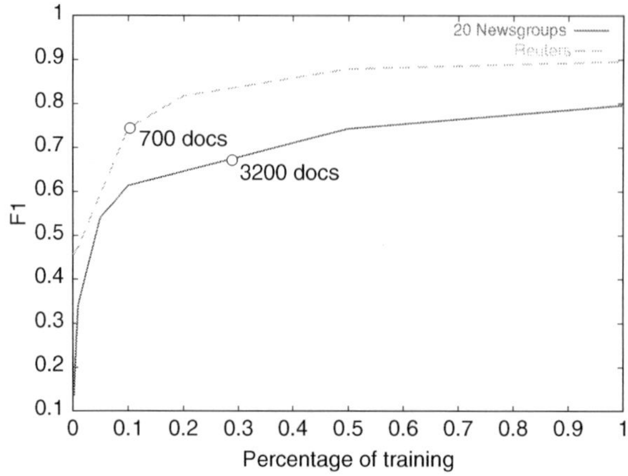

Fig. 4.5. *Extensional* learning curves as percentage of the training set

Comparison with Other Algorithms

As mentioned earlier it is not easy to conduct a thorough comparison with other algorithms in the literature. Most IL data sets used for training and evaluation are either not available [61] or are composed by somewhat arbitrary subsets of a standard data set. Another crucial aspect is the particular choice of the seed terms selected to compose an ID, which significantly affects the overall performance of the algorithm.

As a baseline system, we implemented a rule-based approach in the spirit of [61]. It is based on two steps. First, all the documents in the unlabeled training corpus containing at least one word in common with one and only one category ID are assigned to the respective class. Second, a supervised classifier based on SVM is trained on the labeled examples. Finally, the supervised classifier is used to perform the final categorization step on the test corpus. Table 4.5 reports the F1 measure of our replication of this method, using the category name as seed, which is substantially lower than the performance of the method we presented in this chapter.

Table 4.5. Rule-based baseline performance

	Reuters	*20-Newsgroups*
	0.34	0.30
+ *bootstrap*	0.42	0.47

We also tried to replicate two of the non-standard data sets used in [54].[11] Table 4.6 displays the performance of our approach in comparison to the results reported in [54]. Following the evaluation metric adopted in that paper we report here accuracy instead of F1. For each data set [54] reported several results varying the number of seed words (from 5 to 30), as well as varying some heuristic thresholds, so in the table we report their best results. Notably, our method obtained comparable accuracy by using just the category name as ID for each class instead of multiple seed terms. This result suggests that our method enables to avoid the somewhat fuzzy process of collecting manually a substantial number of additional seed words.

Table 4.6. Accuracy on four "REC" and four "TALK" newsgroups categories

	Our	*IDs per cat.*	*Liu et al.*	*IDs per cat.*
REC	0.94	1	0.95	5
TALK	0.80	1	0.80	20

4.2.4 Discussion

We presented a general bootstrapping algorithm for IL. The algorithm can be applied to any categorization problem in which categories are described by initial sets of discriminative features and an unlabeled training data set is provided. Our algorithm utilizes the Domain Kernel to improve the similarity estimation and a GM algorithm as a principled method to scale similarity scores into probabilities. Both techniques address inherent limitations of the IL setting, and leverage unsupervised information from an unlabeled corpus.

We applied and evaluated our algorithm on some Text Categorization tasks and showed the contribution of the two techniques. In particular, we obtain, for the first time, competitive performance using only the category names as initial seeds. Interesting results were revealed when comparing our IL method to a state-of-the-art extensional classifier, trained on manually labeled documents. The Extensional Learning classifier required 70 (*Reuters-10* data set) or 160 (*20-Newsgroups* data set) documents per category to achieve the same performance that IL obtained using only the category names. These results suggest that IL may provide an appealing cost-effective alternative when sub-optimal accuracy suffices, or when it is too costly or impractical to obtain sufficient labeled training. Optimal combination of extensional and intensional supervision is raised as a challenging topic for future research.

[11] We used sequential splitting (70/30) rather than random splitting and did not apply any feature selection. This setting might be somewhat more difficult than the original one.

4.3 Summary

In this chapter we claimed that the VSM representation for texts allows us to capture relevant distinctions required to perform topic similarity estimations among texts, while other types of analysis seem totally irrelevant for this task. This representation can be further improved by defining a Domain Space, in which classes of coherent terms are mapped into common dimensions, with the effect of avoiding (partially) the problems of ambiguity, variability and sparseness, affecting the VSM. On the basis of these observations, we defined the Domain Kernel, as a way to implement a semi-supervised learning schema that can be applied to any task in which a topic similarity estimation is required.

It has been shown that the Domain Kernel allows a better generalization over the training data than a standard BoW approach, improving substantially the learning curve of the learning algorithm in all the tasks to which it has been applied. We concentrated on the Text Categorization task, in which the problem of topic similarity is fundamental. The task has been approached in the framework of Kernel Methods, following a supervised methodology.

In addition we proposed an IL schema that we applied to the problem of term-based Text Categorization, in which relevant terms for each category are provided instead of relevant texts. Even in this case, the Domain Kernel have been successfully adopted, exploiting the duality property of the Domain Space.

Good classification performance, obtained by using a limited amount of training data, suggests that the notion of DM represents a viable model for human understanding of topic similarity. In fact, the human capability in solving the same tasks is similar to the algorithm performance, demonstrating the high quality of the domain modeling in topic similarity.

From an analysis of the results, it seems evident that domain relations among words, represented by means of DMs, are enough to estimate topic similarity, while deeper semantic relations (e.g. hyponymy, synonymy) seem redundant, and then they should not be modeled to solve such tasks. DMs can be easily acquired from unlabeled corpora describing the application scenarios, with the practical effect of reducing the overall development cost of the final application.

5

Semantic Domains in Word Sense Disambiguation

As far as lexical ambiguity is concerned, Semantic Domains may be considered from two points of view: (i) as a linguistic notion, that can be modeled independently, and then applied uniformly to describe sense distinctions for any word in the lexicon; and (ii) as a useful coarse grained level of sense distinction, to be profitably used in a wide range of applications that do not require the finer grained sense distinctions typically reported in dictionaries.

A major portion of the information required for sense disambiguation corresponds to domain relations among words. Many of the features that contribute to disambiguation identify the domains that characterize a particular sense or subset of senses. For example, economics terms provide characteristic features for the financial senses of words like bank and interest, while legal terms characterize the judicial sense of sentence and court.

Common supervised WSD methods capture such domain-related distinctions separately for each word, by adopting BoW features to represent the context in which the word to be disambiguated occurs, and may require relatively many training examples in order to obtain sufficiently many features of this kind for each sense [98]. The problem of identifying domain-specific senses is then usually approached as a Text Categorization problem (see Sect. 4.1). As discussed in Sect. 3.7.1, such sparse feature representation requires huge amounts of training data to learn the relevant distinctions when applied to Text Categorization tasks. The same problem is even more relevant when the BoW representation is used for WSD. In fact most of the supervised WSD systems approach the task by adopting a word-expert strategy, consisting of training a different classifier for each word to be disambiguated. BoW features are then evidently inadequate in modeling domain distinctions for word senses, because they require a huge amount of sense labeled data for each word in order to train a word expert classifier. This is one of the principal causes of the knowledge acquisition bottleneck in WSD, discussed in Sect. 5.2.

However, domains represent an independent linguistic notion of discourse, which does not depend on a specific word sense. Therefore, it is beneficial to model a relatively small number of domains directly, as a generalized notion,

A. Gliozzo and C. Strapparava, *Semantic Domains in Computational Linguistics*,
DOI: 10.1007/978-3-540-68158-8_5, © Springer-Verlag Berlin Heidelberg 2009

and then use the same generalized information for many instances of the WSD task. A major goal of this chapter is to study the extent to which domain information can contribute along this vein to WSD.

In addition domains may provide a useful coarse-grained level of sense distinction. Many applications do not benefit from fine grained sense distinctions (such as WordNet synsets), which are often impossible to detect by WSD within practical applications (e.g. some verbs in WordNet have more than 40 sense distinctions). However, applications such as Information Retrieval [34] and User Modeling for news web sites [57] can benefit from sense distinctions at the domain level, which are substantially easier to establish in practical WSD.

In this chapter we will present and evaluate both unsupervised and supervised WSD approaches that rely on the notion of Semantic Domain. The former is based on the lexical resource WordNet Domains and the latter exploits both sense tagged and unlabeled data to model the relevant domain distinctions among word senses. At the moment, both techniques achieve the state-of-the-art in WSD. The chapter is structured as follows. In Sect. 5.1 the WSD task is presented, and some evaluation measures are reported. Then, in Sect. 5.2, we will concentrate on the Knowledge Acquisition Bottleneck problem in WSD, identifying the domain-based approach as a viable solution for it. In Sect. 5.3 a literature review about using domain information for WSD is provided. Finally, two WSD systems exploiting domain information are described: Domain-Driven Disambiguation (see Sect. 5.4) and Kernel WSD (see Sect. 5.5).

5.1 The Word Sense Disambiguation Task

Lexical disambiguation is at the basis of text understanding, and should be performed by any NLP system to allow a deep semantic analysis of the text. The WSD task is to assign the correct sense to a word in context from a predefined sense repository. In the typical WSD framework, the relevant sense distinctions for the words to be disambiguated are illustrated by means of dictionary definitions.

A WSD system is usually required as a component of more complex systems to allow further semantic analysis. In fact, disambiguating words in texts is a way to link those words to the concepts of an external ontology, allowing the NLP systems to exploit the additional information there contained. It has been claimed that many NLP systems would benefit from an accurate WSD system. In particular Information Retrieval and Machine Translation are two NLP applications where WSD has brought about improvement in accuracy: when tested on some standard Information Retrieval test collection, the use of WSD improves precision by about 4.3% points [79]; [18] has successfully used WSD to improve the accuracy of Machine Translation. These examples clearly demonstrate the utility of WSD in practical NLP applications. The main limitation of the present WSD technology is the low accuracy reported by most of the systems when it asked them to disambiguate any word in the language. A high accuracy is a fundamental requisite of any WSD system in order to be profitably used in most of the NLP applications.

The literature has distinguished between supervised and unsupervised approaches to WSD. Supervised approaches rely on the availability of sense labeled data, from which the relevant sense distinctions are learned, while unsupervised WSD typically refers to disambiguating word senses without the use of sense-tagged corpora.[1] Most of the unsupervised approaches proposed in the WSD literature are knowledge-based, i.e. they exploit only the information provided by a machine readable dictionary [52, 2]. Some unsupervised WSD systems also use unlabeled data together with the dictionary information to perform an unsupervised learning step [62]. A more recent research direction in WSD is the semi-supervised approach, consisting of providing labeled data together with unlabeled data [29]. In this chapter we will propose both a semi-supervised and an unsupervised WSD algorithm that strongly relies on the notion of Semantic Domain.

In general, the best performances are achieved by supervised WSD systems that follows a *word-expert* approach [83, 98], consisting of defining a different classifier for each word to be disambiguated. Large sets of sense tagged examples for each word are then required for training. However this is clearly unfeasible for *all-words* WSD tasks, in which all the words of an open text should be disambiguated (this problem will be discussed into details in Sect. 5.2).

The attention of the NLP community to the WSD task has been attested to the organization of three evaluation campaigns for WSD during the last decade: Senseval-1 [45], Senseval-2 [75] and Senseval-3 [64]. *Senseval*[2] is a contest for evaluating the strengths and weaknesses of WSD systems with respect to different words and different languages. In the spirit of shared tasks, the Senseval evaluation exercises provide a framework to perform a uniform comparison among different WSD techniques. In particular, two different typologies of WSD tasks have been elaborated: lexical sample and all words tasks.[3]

In the Senseval context, some standard evaluation metrics for WSD have been elaborated. In particular precision, recall, coverage and F1. In contrast to the Text Categorization task, in which one or more categories, selected from a common set, are assigned to each text, the WSD tasks adopt different sense

---

[1] The term unsupervised WSD does not necessarily refer to clustering of unlabeled training examples, which is what unsupervised learning traditionally means in machine learning.

[2] `http://www.senseval.org`.

[3] Some variants of the WSD task have been proposed during the Senseval exercise attracting very limited interest, as for example WSD for machine translation, consisting of assigning the appropriate translating terms in a different language to words in context.

repositories for each word and only one sense per word is assigned[4]. These observations had lead the WSD community to propose a modified formulation for the evaluation metrics already mentioned, reported below:

$$\text{precision} = \frac{\text{GOOD}}{\text{GOOD} + \text{BAD}} \tag{5.1}$$

$$\text{recall} = \frac{\text{GOOD}}{\text{GOOD} + \text{BAD} + \text{NULL}} \tag{5.2}$$

$$\text{coverage} = \frac{\text{GOOD} + \text{BAD}}{\text{GOOD} + \text{BAD} + \text{NULL}} \tag{5.3}$$

where GOOD is the number of correct sense assignments, BAD is the number of uncorrected ones and NULL is the number of word occurrences to which the algorithm did not provide any answer.[5]

These figures can be evaluated once a "gold standard" data set [44] (i.e. a manually annotated sense tagged corpus) is provided. The main requisite of a gold standard is a high inter-tagger agreement (i.e. the percentage of times in which two different lexicographers agree on the sense assignment in a given corpus and with respect to a given dictionary). [44] claims that the inter-tagger agreement defines the upper-bound for how well a computer program can perform. It has been asserted that if a two humans agrees only 80% of times, then it is not clear what it means to say that a WSD program was more than 80% accurate.[6]

The lower-bound for a WSD task can be established by evaluating the performance of a baseline system on the gold standard data set. A *baseline* is a naive algorithm that exploits the same training data and lexical resources available to the WSD algorithm to which it is compared. In the WSD literature different baselines have been proposed for supervised and unsupervised WSD algorithms. The most commonly used baseline to evaluate supervised WSD systems is the most frequent heuristic, consisting on assigning the sense having the highest frequency to all the occurrences of each word.[7] On the other hand, the random baseline is typically used to evaluate unsupervised

[4] In principle, some word occurrences could be disambiguated by selecting more than one sense. In practice, it is more convenient to force the WSD system to select only the most likely sense for each word occurrence. This last solution is the most commonly adopted.

[5] In the literature some modified formulations to estimate precision and recall have been proposed, to allow multiple sense assignments for each word occurrence [77].

[6] On the other hand, the more recent supervised systems for WSD outperformed this upper bound, re-opening an old controversial philosophical discussion in Artificial Intelligence: can a computer perform better than a human? In this book, we do not provide any solution to this dilemma, limiting ourselves to report some empirical observations.

[7] The frequency estimation is performed on the sense tagged corpus available for training.

WSD systems. A more complex unsupervised WSD baseline is the Lesk algorithm [52], consisting of counting the number of words in common between the dictionary entries and the contexts of the words to be disambiguated. It is typically used to evaluate memory-based WSD systems. In its supervised version the Lesk algorithm[8] is also used as a baseline for supervised WSD systems. Typically, the baselines are evaluated by the organizers of the WSD tasks, together with the inter-tagger agreement, to provide upper and lower bounds to compare the systems' performances.

As far as the WSD accuracy is concerned, supervised approaches are far better than unsupervised ones, allowing us to achieve performances that are very close to the upper bound in many tasks. On the other hand, unsupervised approaches do not require labeled training data, allowing us to design cheap and portable WSD methodologies, that can be easily adapted to the particular application domain by simply providing a dictionary and/or an unlabeled corpus.

5.2 The Knowledge Acquisition Bottleneck in Supervised WSD

In the previous section we introduced the WSD task and we identified the supervised approach as the more accurate way to design WSD systems. On the other hand, the main limitation of most of the supervised approaches in NLP is the lack of available annotated training data. Algorithms designed for lexical sample WSD are often based on pure supervision and hence "data hungry". For example [69] estimated that, in order to surpass the most frequent baseline by adopting the available supervised WSD technology, a sense tagged corpus of 3.2 words would be required for training. In the same work, it has also been estimated that the annotation of such a corpus would require about 16 man years work. It is then a common opinion that the performance of state-of-the-art WSD systems is not satisfactory from an applicative point of view yet. In fact, even if, in principle, it would be possible to collect such a corpus, it could be used only to train the WSD systems with respect to a particular dictionary in a given language. In practice, different application scenarios often require different sense distinctions, making infeasible such a huge annotation procedure, due to the very high annotation costs required. This problem is known as the Knowledge Acquisition Bottleneck.

By the way, minimal supervision is the basis of state-of-the-art systems for all-words tasks (e.g. [65, 21]), that are trained on small sense tagged corpora (e.g. SemCor), in which few examples for a subset of the ambiguous words in the lexicon can be found. Thus, improving the WSD performance with few

---

[8] The supervised Lesk algorithm consists of counting the number of words in common among the context of the word to be disambiguated and the sense tagged examples.

learning is a fundamental issue to be solved to design supervised WSD system working on real texts.

To achieve these goals, we identified two promising research directions:

1. Modeling independently domain and syntagmatic aspects of sense distinction, to improve the feature representation of sense tagged examples [32].
2. Leveraging external knowledge acquired from unlabeled corpora [29].

The first direction is motivated by the linguistic assumption that syntagmatic and domain (associative) relations are both crucial to represent sense distinctions, while they are basically originated by very different phenomena. Syntagmatic relations hold among words that are typically located close to each other in the same sentence in a given temporal order, while domain relations hold among words that are typically used in the same Semantic Domain (i.e. in texts having similar topics [32]). Their different nature suggests adopting different learning strategies to detect them.

Regarding the second direction, external knowledge would be required to help WSD algorithms to better generalize over the data available for training. On the other hand, most of the state-of-the-art supervised approaches to WSD are still completely based on "internal" information only (i.e. the only information available to the training algorithm is the set of manually annotated examples). For example, in the Senseval-3 evaluation exercise [64] many lexical sample tasks were provided, beyond the usual labeled training data, with a large set of unlabeled data. The original intention of the organizers was to promote the development of semi-supervised learning techniques in WSD. However, to our knowledge, none of the participants exploited this unlabeled material. In this work we will exploit such information to model domain information independently from the particular word to be disambiguated, in such a way to acquire once for all the relevant domain distinctions by adopting unsupervised learning techniques. In Sect. 5.5 we will show that domain information can be modeled independently from syntagmatic information, allowing us to design weakly supervised learning algorithms for WSD.

5.3 Semantic Domains in the WSD Literature

In the NLP literature the exploitation of Semantic Domains has been shown to be fruitful for sense disambiguation (e.g. the pioneering works of [35, 96]). [35] exploited the *subject-codes* supplementary fields of LDOCE. In addition to using the Lesk-based method of counting overlaps between definitions and contexts, they imposed a correspondence of subject codes in an iterative process. [96] bases WSD on the 1042 categories of Roget's Thesaurus. The idea underlying the algorithm is that different word senses tend to belong to different conceptual classes, and such classes tend to appear in recognizably different contexts. From a technical point of view, the correct subject category is estimated maximizing the sum of a Bayesian term ($\log \frac{\Pr(\text{word}|\text{RCat})}{\Pr(\text{word})}$, i.e. the probability of a word appearing in a context of a Roget category divided by its overall probability in the corpus) over all possible subject categories for the ambiguous word in its context (± 50 words). Thus, identifying the conceptual class of a context provides a crucial clue for discriminating word senses that belong to that class. The results were promising, the system correctly disambiguated 92% of the instances of 12 polysemous words on Grolier's Encyclopedia. [84] use the LDOCE subject codes by adapting the Yarowsky algorithm. Experiments were performed on a subset of the British National Corpus (BNC) on the words appearing at least 10 times in the training context of a particular word. In addition, while [96] assumed a uniform prior probability for each Roget category, the probability of each subject category was estimated as the proportion of senses in LDOCE to which a given category was assigned.

More recently, [58] and [32] presented a system completely based on domain information at Senseval-2. The underlying hypothesis of the *Domain-Driven Disambiguation* approach is that information provided by domain labels offers a natural way to establish associations among word senses in a certain text fragment, which can be profitably used during the disambiguation process. In Sect. 5.4 we will describe this algorithm in detail.

An alternative way to represent domain information in WSD is to provide domain features to a supervised learning algorithm. As described in Sect. 3.7, providing BoW features is the easiest way to model domain distinctions explicitly. Thus, most of the supervised approaches to WSD model domain distinctions separately for each word, by providing BoW features for a large context of the word to be disambiguated [98]. Another solution is to model domain features for the context of the word to be disambiguated explicitly, by exploiting an external knowledge source that represents an "a-priori" association among words and a domain set, and by representing the relevance of each domain as an explicit feature for the example. This approach has been followed by [24], which used domain features, explicitly extracted for each example to be disambiguated, by exploiting the information from WordNet Domains in a supervised classification setting tested on the Senseval-2 tasks. The introduction of such domain features systematically improved the system performance, especially for nouns (over three percentage points of improvement).

In a more recent work [32], a wide comparison between BoW and domain features has been performed in a supervised framework, demonstrating that the exploitation of domain features improves sensibly the learning curve. The more recent elaboration of this approach has been proposed in [29], which exploited a Domain Kernel (see Sect. 3.7) to model domain distinctions in a supervised framework, obtaining the state-of-the-art in several lexical sample tasks of the Senseval-3 competition [64]. In Sect. 5.5 we will describe this approach in detail.

5.4 Domain-Driven Disambiguation

Domain-Driven Disambiguation (DDD) [59] is a generic WSD methodology that utilizes only domain information to perform WSD. For this reason DDD is not able to capture sense distinctions that depend on syntagmatic relations, while it represents a viable WSD methodology to perform a domain grained WSD, that can be profitably used by a wide range of applications, such as Information Retrieval and User Modeling [57]. DDD can be performed in a totally unsupervised way once a set of relevant domains has been associated to each sense of the word to be disambiguated. In this section we evaluate the DDD methodology in an "all-words" task (see Subsect. 5.4.2), for which sense tagged data are not provided for learning. In addition we evaluate the performances of DDD on both a domain grained and sense grained WSD task, with the aim of demonstrating its applicability to real NLP applications.

5.4.1 Methodology

The basic problems to be solved to design a lexical disambiguation algorithm based on Semantic Domains are: (i) to associate domain information to each sense of the word to be disambiguated; (ii) to recognize the domain of the context in which the word occurs. Obviously, exactly the same domain set should be adopted to solve both problems, in order to allow a homogenous comparison. These problems are then intimately connected, and can be approached in several ways, depending on the available lexical resources.

The DDD algorithm implements the ideas already described. For each occurrence of an ambiguous word w, DDD is basically performed in the following three steps:

- Compute the DV $\mathbf{t'}$ for the text window t of $\pm h$ tokens around the occurrence of the word w to be disambiguated.[9]
- Compute $\hat{c} = \text{argmax}_{c \in \text{Senses}(w)} \text{score}(c, w, t)$ where

$$\text{score}(c, w, t) = \frac{P(c|w) \cdot \langle \mathbf{c'}, \mathbf{t'} \rangle}{\sum_{c_i \in \text{Senses}(w)} P(c_i|w) \cdot \langle \mathbf{c'_i}, \mathbf{t'} \rangle}$$

  and $\mathbf{c'}$ is the DV associated to c and $P(c|w)$ describes the prior probability of a sense c for the word w, which may depend on the distribution of senses in the target corpus.[10]

---

[9] In our experiments the parameter h has been fixed empirically at 50, following [26].

[10] In the experiments reported in this section, we estimated these probabilities based on frequency counts in the generally available SemCor corpus. Admittedly, this may be regarded as a supervised component within the generally unsupervised system version. However, we considered this component as legitimate within a typical unsupervised setting since it relies on a general resource (SemCor) that

- if score$(\hat{c}, w, t) \geqslant \theta$ (where $\theta \in [0, 1]$ is a confidence threshold) select sense $\hat{c}$, else do not provide any answer.

The DDD methodology can be implemented in several ways, depending on the particular algorithm adopted to estimate the DVs $\mathbf{c}'$ for the senses c of the word w to be disambiguated and the DV $\mathbf{t}'$ describing the context t in which it occurs. In our implementation the DVs $\mathbf{c}'$ are obtained from WordNet Domains, by estimating the domain relevance $R(D, c)$ of the concept c with respect to each domain D in the domain set $\mathcal{D}$ of WordNet Domains. This operation is performed by exploiting Eq. 3.2. In addition, we adopt the IL algorithm for Text Categorization (see Sect. 4.2) to estimate the DV $\mathbf{t}'$ for the context t of the word to be disambiguated. In the WSD settings, the domain set $\mathcal{D}$ is adopted, and a list of seed words for each domain is obtained by collecting all the corresponding domain-specific words. Given the high number of seed words provided by WordNet Domains, the similarity is estimated in the Text VSM and no bootstrap phase is done. The parameters required to learn the GM algorithm have been estimated by using the texts contained in the BNC corpus. Equation 4.1 is then iteratively applied to estimate the domain relevance for all the domains D in the domain set $\mathcal{D}$ with respect to the context t of the word to be disambiguated, to obtain a DV $\mathbf{t}'$ containing the probability for each domain to be relevant for the text.[11]

5.4.2 Evaluation

Evaluation Task

The DDD system has been tested on the *Senseval-2 English all-words task*: the test data consists of 5000 words of running text from three Penn Treebank II Wall Street Journal articles. The total number of words to be disambiguated is 2473. Sense tags are assigned using WordNet 1.7. Training examples are not provided in this collection. The DDD system was evaluated using both sense and domain grained distinctions.

Domain Grained Versus Sense Grained Evaluation

Figure 5.1 shows the precision/coverage curves of the system at both granularity levels. At full coverage, the domain level precision is 0.83 compared to 0.62 for sense granularity. This result assesses the practical effectiveness of DDD for domain level granularity in unsupervised settings. For sense granularity the DDD system achieves good precision levels only at relatively low

does not correspond to the test data and task, as in the all-words task. This setting is distinguished from having quite a few annotated training examples that are provided by construction for each test sense in a supervised setting, as in the lexical sample task.

11 Details of the domain relevance estimation technique are reported in our previous work [30, 32].

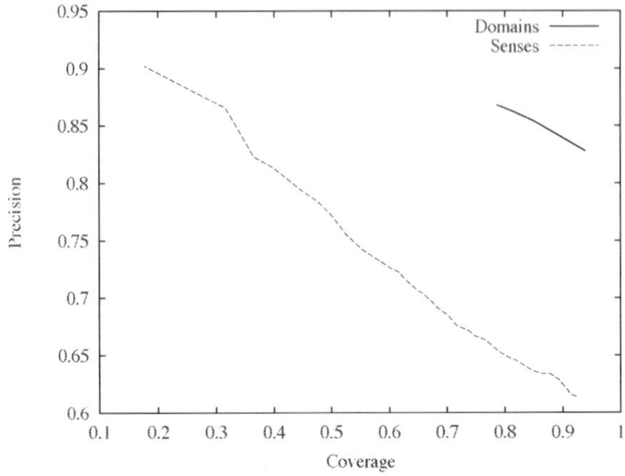

Fig. 5.1. Precision/coverage curve in the Senseval-2 English all-words task (both domain and sense grained)

coverage (0.86 precision at 0.3 coverage). Domain-level senses provide an appealing coarse granularity for WSD. Disambiguation at the domain level is substantially more accurate, while the accuracy of WSD for the fine-grained sense-level may not be good enough for various applications. Disambiguation at domain granularity is accurate and can be sufficiently practical using only domain information with the unsupervised DDD method alone, even with no training examples.

Sense Grained Evaluation

Table 5.1. All-words sense grained results by PoS

	Prec	Rec	Coverage	F1
nouns	0.626	0.613	0.980	0.620
verbs	0.437	0.434	0.993	0.435
adj	0.601	0.584	0.971	0.592
adv	0.756	0.753	0.996	0.754

The performance of DDD for sense granularity was also evaluated separately for each PoS. Results are reported in Table 5.1. As assumed, the system is not so accurate for verbs, but it achieves satisfactory results for the remaining PoSs. In particular the system achieves a good F1 figure for nouns, which is very close to state-of-the-art results obtained by more complex supervised systems that use labeled training data.[12]

[12] See [75] for a comparison among all systems on the Senseval-2 all-words task.

Comparison to the State-of-the-Art

For comparison, Table 5.2 reports results for the standard "most frequent" baseline, as well as for two Senseval-2 all-words systems that exploit the notion of Semantic Domains, even though not necessarily using WORDNET DOMAINS information. Sinequa LIA-HMM exploits statistical models to identify some coarse semantic classes related to each word in the test, while DIMAP exploits the idea of topical area matches (see [75] and the Senseval Web site for more information about these systems).

	Precision	Coverage
Sinequa LIA	0.61	1.0
DIMAP	0.45	1.0
Most frequent	0.605	1.0

Table 5.2. Performances of systems that utilize the notion of Semantic Domains on the Senseval-2 English all-words task

5.5 Domain Kernels for WSD

In the previous section we described the DDD methodology, demonstrating that domain information is crucial to perform WSD, even if it is not enough to disambiguate all the words in the lexicon. In fact, word senses can also be distinguished by syntagmatic relations, that should be recognized from an analysis of the word sequences in the local context of the word to be disambiguated. To take into account these aspects of lexical ambiguity, WSD systems should deal with both collocations and syntactic constraints.

In this section we describe *Kernel WSD*, a supervised WSD algorithm that takes into account both domain and syntagmatic aspects of sense distinctions at the same time. Kernel WSD is designed in the framework of Kernel Methods; then it is fully defined by a kernel function. Such a function should be able to estimate the similarity among the contexts in which the word to be disambiguated occurs (see Appendix A). The kernel function implemented by Kernel WSD estimates the similarity among two contexts by taking into account both domain and syntagmatic aspects. Domain and syntagmatic relations are modeled differently because they show inherently different behaviors. To this end, Kernel WSD exploits a kernel combination schema, consisting on defining the kernel function to be used for classification by means of a linear combination of n basic different kernels. Each kernel adds some additional dimension to the feature space, taking into account the different aspects of sense distinction independently.

In particular, we have defined two families of kernels: *Domain* and *Syntagmatic* kernels. The former is composed by both the Domain Kernel (K_D) and the BoW kernel (K_{BoW}), that capture domain aspects (see Sect. 3.7). The latter estimate syntagmatic aspects of sense distinction by means of String Kernels measuring the similarities among sequences of PoSs (K_{PoS}) and lemmata (K_{Coll}) in the local context of the word to be disambiguated (see Subsect. 5.5.2). The final kernel, namely K_{WSD}, is then defined by combining them (see Subsect. 5.5.3). Finally in Subsect. 5.5.4 we extensively evaluate the Kernel WSD system in four lexical sample tasks.

5.5.1 The Domain Kernel

A viable way to represent domain information for WSD is to provide domain features to a supervised learning algorithm (see Sect. 3.7.1). In the framework of Kernel Methods, such an operation can be performed implicitly by defining a Domain Kernel. The Domain Kernel estimates the similarity among the contexts in which the word occurs in the Domain Space, defined by exploiting the information provided by a DM. In Sect. 3.7 we extensively described the Domain Kernel, showing that it is able to estimate the topic similarity among two texts in a way that both variability and ambiguity are taken into account. In this section we will exploit exactly the same kernel to approach the WSD task.

To be fully defined, the Domain Kernel requires a DM, that can be automatically acquired from unlabeled data in a totally unsupervised way. In the WSD settings, we acquire the DM from large scale unlabeled text collections, and we use such information in the supervised framework to estimate the topic similarity among the large contexts in which the word to be disambiguated occurs. The DM, acquired from unlabeled data, is then an external knowledge source to be used by the supervised learning algorithm. Using the Domain Kernel as a component of a WSD system is then a way to define a semi-supervised learning schema for WSD.

The use of the Domain Kernel in WSD is motivated by the same underlying assumptions that have led us to the definition of the DDD algorithm. In fact, the Domain Kernel estimates the domain of the context of the word to be disambiguated and compares it to the domain of each word sense. In contrast with it, the Domain Kernel acquires a DM from unlabeled data and learns the relevant domains for each sense by performing a supervised learning step. In this way, it is possible to avoid the use of WordNet Domains, so to define a totally corpus-based DDD schema.

As discussed in the previous chapter, a simpler way to model domain distinctions is to compare the similarities among the contexts of the word to be disambiguated in the Text VSM. This simpler model does not take into account second order relations among terms, and is implemented by means of the BoW Kernel, denoted by K_{BoW}.

5.5.2 Syntagmatic Kernels

Syntagmatic relations hold among words collocated in a particular temporal order, then they have to be modeled by analyzing word sequences. State-of-the-art WSD systems model such relations by including in the feature set bigrams and trigrams in a local context of the word to be disambiguated. The main drawback of this approach is that non-contiguous or shifted collocations cannot be identified, decreasing the generalization power of the learning algorithm. For example, suppose that the verb `to score` has to be disambiguated into the sentence "Ronaldo *scored* the goal", and that the sense tagged example "the football player scores#1 the first goal" is provided for training. A traditional feature mapping would extract the bigram `w+1+2:the_goal` to represent the former, and the bigram `w+1+2:the_first` to index the latter. Evidently such features will not match, leading the algorithm to a misclassification.

To solve these problems, we adopted a Gap-Weighted Subsequence Kernel [81] to model syntagmatic relations. In the spirit of Kernel Methods, this kernel is able to compare sequences directly in the input space, avoiding any explicit feature mapping. To perform this operation, it counts how many times a (non-contiguous) subsequence of symbols u of length n occurs in the input string s, and penalizes non-contiguous occurrences according to the number of gaps they contain. For more details see Appendix A.6.

We adapted the generic definition of this kernel to the problem of recognizing collocations in a local window of the word to be disambiguated. In particular we defined two Syntagmatic Kernels: the *n-gram* Collocation Kernel and the *n-gram* PoS Kernel. The *n-gram* Collocation kernel K^n_{Coll} is defined as a Gap-Weighted Subsequence Kernel applied to sequences of lemmata around the word l_0 to be disambiguated (i.e. $s = l_{-3}, l_{-2}, l_{-1}, l_0, l_{+1}, l_{+2}, l_{+3}$, where l_0 is the position of the word to be disambiguated). This formulation allows us to estimate the number of common (sparse) subsequences of lemmata (i.e. collocations) between two examples, in order to capture syntagmatic similarity. In analogy we defined the PoS kernel K^n_{PoS} by applying a Gap-Weighted Subsequence Kernel to the sequence of PoSs $s = p_{-3}, p_{-2}, p_{-1}, p_0, p_{+1}, p_{+2}, p_{+3}$, where p_0 is the PoS of the word to be disambiguated.

The definition of the Gap-Weighted Subsequence Kernel, provided by Eq. A.36, depends on the parameter n, that represents the number of tokens in the subsequences adopted as features. For example, K^2_{Coll} counts the number of sparse bigrams in common to the local contexts around the words to be disambiguated.

In WSD, typical features are bigrams and trigrams of lemmata and PoSs around the word to be disambiguated; then we defined the Collocation Kernel and the PoS Kernel respectively by Eq. 5.4 and 5.5:

$$K_{\text{Coll}}(s_i, s_j) = \sum_{l=1}^{p} K^l_{\text{Coll}}(s_i, s_j) \tag{5.4}$$

$$K_{\mathrm{PoS}}(s_i, s_j) = \sum_{l=1}^{p} K^l_{\mathrm{PoS}}(s_i, s_j) \tag{5.5}$$

The parameters p and λ are optimized by cross-validation. For example, in the English Lexical Sample Task (see Subsect. 5.5.4) we obtained the best results setting $p = 2$, $\lambda = 0.5$ for K_{Coll} and $p = 2$, $\lambda \to 0$ for K_{PoS}.

5.5.3 WSD Kernels

In order to show the impact of using DMs in the supervised learning process, we defined two WSD Kernels, by applying the following kernel combination schema (see Appendix A for more details):

$$K_C(x_i, x_j) = \sum_{l=1}^{n} \frac{K_l(x_i, x_j)}{\sqrt{K_l(x_j, x_j) K_l(x_i, x_i)}} \tag{5.6}$$

Thus, the WSD kernels are fully specified by the lists of the kernels that compose them.

$\mathbf{K_{wsd}}$ composed by K_{Coll}, K_{PoS} and K_{BoW};
$\mathbf{K'_{wsd}}$ composed by K_{Coll}, K_{PoS}, K_{BoW} and K_D.

The only difference between the two systems is that K'_{wsd} uses the Domain Kernel K_D. K'_{wsd} is then a semi-supervised WSD system, because it exploits external knowledge acquired from unlabeled data, in contrast to K_{wsd} that only exploits the available labeled training data.

5.5.4 Evaluation

In this section we report the evaluation we did of our kernel-based algorithms for WSD. The objectives of these experiments are:

- to estimate the impact of different knowledge sources in WSD;
- to study the effectiveness of the kernel combination schema;
- to understand the benefits of plugging external information by using DMs in a supervised framework;
- to verify the portability of our methodology among different languages.

WSD Tasks

We conducted the experiments on four lexical sample tasks (English, Catalan, Italian and Spanish) of the Senseval-3 competition [64]. Table 5.3 describes the tasks by reporting the number of words to be disambiguated, the mean polysemy, and the dimension of training, test and unlabeled corpora. Note that the organizers of the English task did not provide any unlabeled material. So for English we used a DM acquired from the analysis of a portion of the BNC corpus, while for Spanish, Italian and Catalan we acquired the DMs from the unlabeled corpora made available by the organizers.

Table 5.3. Senseval-3 lexical sample task descriptions

	#w	mean polysemy	# train	# test	# unlab
Catalan	27	3.11	4469	2253	23935
English	57	6.47	7860	3944	-
Italian	45	6.30	5145	2439	74788
Spanish	46	3.30	8430	4195	61252

Kernel Combination

Here we present an experiment to empirically study the impact of different knowledge sources for WSD, and the effectiveness of the kernel combination schema here proposed. The basic kernels (i.e. K_{BoW}, K_{D}, K_{Coll} and K_{PoS}) have been compared to the combined ones (i.e. K_{wsd} and K'_{wsd}) on the English lexical sample task.

Table 5.4. The performance (F1) of each basic kernel and their combination for English lexical sample task

	K_{D}	K_{BoW}	K_{PoS}	K_{Coll}	K_{wsd}	K'_{wsd}
F1	65.5	63.7	62.9	66.7	**69.7**	**73.3**

The results are reported in Table 5.4. They shows that both Syntagmatic Information (captured by K_{Coll}) and Domain Information (captured by K_{D}) are crucial for WSD. In addition the Domain Kernel performs better than the BoW kernel, demonstrating our assumption. Domain features are then more expressive than BoWs.

The results show that combining kernels significantly improves the performance of the system: adding a new kernel to the combination never affects the overall results negatively. In addition the accuracy of the combined kernel was never below the accuracy of the best individual kernel involved in the combination, demonstrating the effectiveness of the kernel combination schema here proposed.

Portability and Performance

We evaluated the performance of K'_{wsd} and K_{wsd} on all the lexical sample tasks described above. The results are shown in Table 5.5 and indicate that using DMs allowed K'_{wsd} to significantly outperform K_{wsd} for all the tasks. In addition, K'_{wsd} turns out to be the best system for all the tested Senseval-3 tasks, improving the state-of-the-art by 0.4% F1 for English to 8.2% F1 for

Table 5.5. Comparative evaluation on the lexical sample tasks. Columns report: the *Most Frequent* baseline, the *inter-annotator agreement*, the *F1* of the best system at Senseval-3, the *F1* of K_{wsd}, and the *F1* of K'_{wsd}, *DM+* (the improvement due to DM, i.e. $K'_{\text{wsd}} - K_{\text{wsd}}$)

	MF	Agreement	BEST	K_{wsd}	K'_{wsd}	DM+
English	55.2	67.3	72.9	69.7	**73.3**	3.6
Catalan	66.3	93.1	85.2	85.2	**89.0**	3.8
Italian	18.0	89.0	53.1	53.1	**61.3**	8.2
Spanish	67.7	85.3	84.2	84.2	**88.2**	4.0

Italian. Finally, the performance of K'_{wsd} is higher than the human agreement for both English and Spanish.[13]

In addition, we demonstrated the language-independence of our approach. In fact, DMs have been acquired for different languages from different unlabeled corpora by adopting exactly the same methodology, without requiring any external lexical resource and ad-hoc rule.

Learning Curves

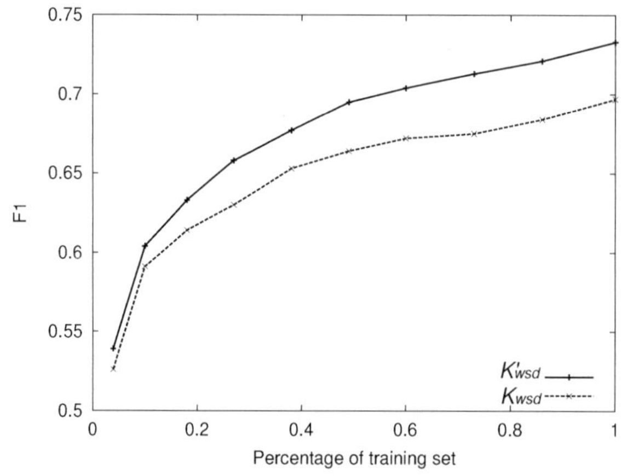

Fig. 5.2. Learning curves for English lexical sample task

[13] In Sect. 5.1 we observed that the inter-annotator agreement is usually regarded as the upper bound for a WSD system. Evidently, this observation is not true. In fact, for the Senseval-3 English lexical sample task, most of the participating systems outperformed the agreement.

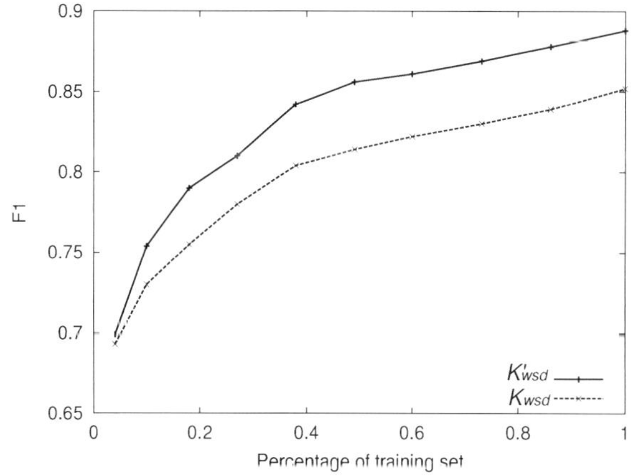

Fig. 5.3. Learning curves for Catalan lexical sample task

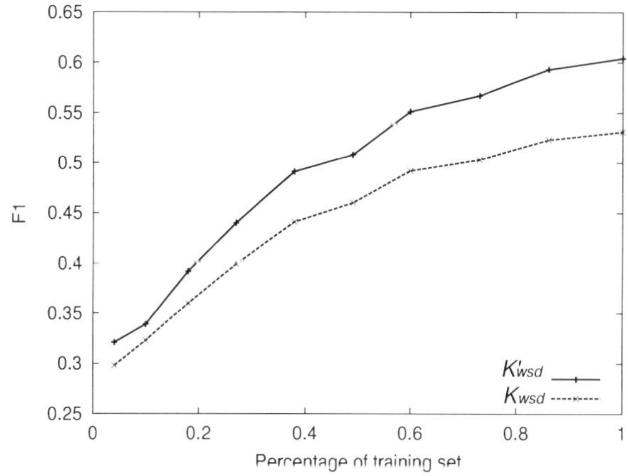

Fig. 5.4. Learning curves for Italian lexical sample task

Table 5.6. Percentage of sense tagged examples required by K'_{wsd} to achieve the same performance of K_{wsd} with full training

	% of training
English	54
Catalan	46
Italian	51
Spanish	50

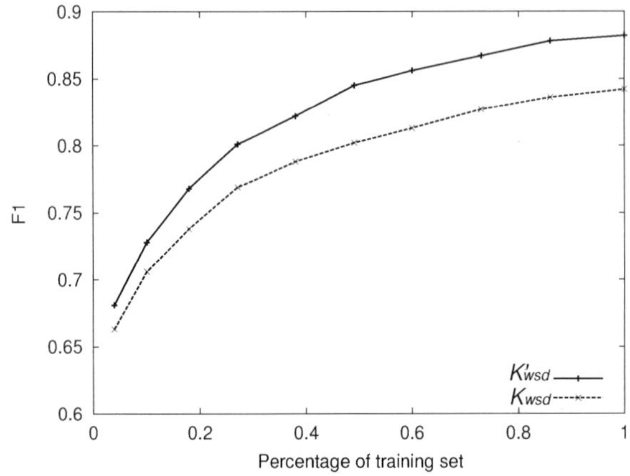

Fig. 5.5. Learning curves for Spanish lexical sample task

The basic motivation that has led us to exploit DMs, acquired from external knowledge sources, in a WSD algorithm has been to reduce the amount of training data required for learning, in order to provide a viable solution for the Knowledge Acquisition Bottleneck in WSD. To demonstrate our assumption, we compared the learning curves of K'_{wsd} and K_{wsd} on four lexical sample tasks. Figures 5.2–5.5 report the results of our experiments. They indicate that K'_{wsd} is far superior to K_{wsd} for all the tasks, even with few examples. The result is extremely promising, for it demonstrates that DMs allow us to drastically reduce the amount of sense tagged data required for learning. It is worth noting, as reported in Table 5.6, that K'_{wsd} achieves the same performance as K_{wsd} using about half of the training data, opening an interesting research direction for all-words tasks, in which the amount of training data is typically very low.

5.6 Discussion

In this chapter we analyzed the role of domain information in WSD, showing that lexical polysemy can be solved by identifying the Semantic Domain in which the word is typically located. The DDD algorithm is mainly based on this intuition. We have shown that it is able to fully disambiguate a subset of the lexicon, consisting of the so called Domain Words, i.e. words whose sense distinctions are mainly due to domain relations. In addition, we have shown that Semantic Domains provide a way to define coarse grained clusters of word senses. We have shown that the DDD algorithm achieves very good accuracy on a domain grained disambiguation task, without requiring any labeled data, providing an effective technology that can be used by NLP applications that do not require finer grained sense distinctions, as for example by search engines.

In the second part of this chapter we discussed the problem of integrating syntagmatic features in our domain-driven WSD approach. To this end we implemented a supervised system, namely Kernel WSD, based on a combination of different kernels, with the aim of measuring different aspects of sense similarity at the same time. Domain relations are then modeled by the Domain Kernel, while syntagmatic relations are independently modeled by a Syntagmatic Kernel, implemented by means of a Gap-Weighted Subsequence Kernel that compares the local contexts in which the word to be disambiguated occur. The Domain Kernel is based on the same underlying assumptions that motivated the definition of the DDD algorithm. It estimates the domain of the contexts in which the word to be disambiguated occurs and compares it to the domain of each sense. In contrast with the DDD approach, the Domain Kernel acquires the DM from unlabeled data, and learns the relevant domains of each sense by means of a supervised learning step. This corpus-based approach is optimal for sense modeling. In fact, the domain set is not fixed in advance, and can be acquired from domain-specific data in order to fit the applicative needs in a more flexible way.

We evaluated our algorithm on several Senseval-3 lexical sample tasks (i.e. English, Spanish, Italian and Catalan) significantly improving the state-of-the-art for all of them. In addition, the performance of our system outperforms the inter-annotator agreement in both English and Spanish, achieving the upper bound performance.

We demonstrated that using external knowledge inside a supervised framework is a viable methodology to reduce the amount of training data required for learning. In our approach the external knowledge is represented by means of DMs automatically acquired from corpora in a totally unsupervised way. Experimental results show that the use of DMs allows us to reduce the amount of training data, opening an interesting research direction to face the Knowledge Acquisition Bottleneck problem in WSD.

The capability of Kernel WSD to learn the sense distinctions with few labeled data in a totally language independent way, and its very high accuracy, makes this technique the present state-of-the-art technology for WSD. Last, but not least, the Domain Kernel has been adopted to uniformly approach both a WSD and a Text Categorization task, demonstrating that domain modeling is a fundamental research direction in Computational Linguistics, and can be studied in a task independent way.

6

Multilingual Domain Models

In the previous chapters we extensively discussed the concept of Semantic Domain in Computational Linguistics, showing that it can be profitably exploited to approach many different NLP tasks in a uniform way. DMs have been conceived in monolingual scenarios, in which domain relations among words in the same language are modeled. On the other hand, as discussed in Sect. 2.1, Semantic Fields are inherently language independent, suggesting that domain relations can be established also among terms in different languages.

In this chapter we will show that the concept of Semantic Domain can be easily extended in order to cope with multilingual scenarios, allowing us to represent domain relations among words in different languages by means of Multilingual Domain Models (MDMs). In fact, as argued in Chap. 2, one of the basic properties of Semantic Domains is their interlinguality. This property allows us to define MDMs (see Sect. 6.1), in which terms in different languages are grouped together and associated to a common domain set. The MDM extends the concept of DM (see Chap. 3) in order to represent the domain similarity among terms in different languages.

MDMs are represented by means of matrices describing the associations among terms in different languages and a common domain set. MDMs can be acquired in several ways, depending on the available lexical resources and corpora. In Sect. 6.6 we will describe several methodologies to acquire MDMs from multilingual corpora, proposing a novel methodology that exploits comparable corpora (see Sect. 6.2) to perform this acquisition task in a totally unsupervised way.

In order to evaluate the acquired MDMs, we defined a Cross-language Text Categorization task, in which we have to cope with two or more languages (e.g. *English* and *Italian*). In this setting, the system is trained using labeled examples in a source language (e.g. *English*) and classification is performed on documents expressed in a different target language (e.g. *Italian*). In this chapter we propose a novel approach to solve the Cross-language Text Categorization task consisting of providing a MDM to a Domain Kernel (see Sect.

A. Gliozzo and C. Strapparava, *Semantic Domains in Computational Linguistics*,
DOI: 10.1007/978-3-540-68158-8_6, © Springer-Verlag Berlin Heidelberg 2009

3.7) in order to define a generalized similarity function among documents in different languages. The Multilingual Domain Kernel is then used inside a SVM classification framework to perform the categorization task. The results show that our approach is a feasible and cheap solution that largely outperforms a baseline.

This chapter is organized as follows. First of all, in Sect. 6.1 we formally introduce the concept of MDM as a viable way to represent domain information in a multilingual scenario. In Sect. 6.2 we discuss the distinction between parallel and comparable corpora, focusing on the former because they represent the basic knowledge source we have adopted to acquire MDMs for our experiments. Then, in Sect. 6.3, we describe a Cross-language Text Categorization task we defined to perform our experiments. In Sect. 6.4 we define both the Multilingual Text VSM and the Multilingual Term VSM, in which documents and terms in different languages can be represented and then compared, showing their basic limitations. These models can be improved by defining a Multilingual Domain Space, illustrated in Sect. 6.5, a vectorial space in which both terms and texts in different languages can be compared taking into account second order domain relations. The Multilingual Domain Kernel, presented in the same section, is simply a similarity function defined in this space. In Sect. 6.6 we illustrate a set of techniques that allow us to acquire MDMs from corpora. Section 6.7 is devoted to evaluating the so obtained cross-language text categorization system. The results show that our approach is a feasible and cheap solution, largely outperforming a baseline. Conclusions and future work are finally reported in Sect. 6.8.

6.1 Multilingual Domain Models: Definition

A MDM is a multilingual extension of the concept of DM, presented in Chap. 3, that allows us to represent domain relations among terms in more than one language. A MDM is represented by a matrix **D**, containing the degree of association among terms in different languages with respect to a common domain set, as illustrated in Table 6.1.

MDMs can be used to describe lexical ambiguity, variability and interlingual domain relations. Lexical ambiguity is represented by associating one term to more than one domain, while variability is represented by associating different terms to the same domain. For example the term *virus* is associated to both the domain COMPUTER_SCIENCE and the domain MEDICINE while the domain MEDICINE is associated to both the terms *AIDS* and *HIV*. Interlingual domain relations are captured by placing different terms of different languages in the same domain (as for example $HIV^{e/i}$, $AIDS^{e/i}$, $hospital^{e}$, and $clinica^{i}$).[1]

[1] It is worth remarking here that most of the named entities, such as *Microsoft*, as well as domain-specific terminology, such as *AIDS* and *HIV*, are expressed by using the same string in both languages.

Table 6.1. Example of MDM. w^e denotes English terms, w^i Italian terms and $w^{e/i}$ the terms common to both languages.

	MEDICINE	COMPUTER_SCIENCE
$HIV^{e/i}$	1	0
$AIDS^{e/i}$	1	0
$virus^{e/i}$	0.5	0.5
$hospital^e$	1	0
$laptop^e$	0	1
$Microsoft^{e/i}$	0	1
$clinica^i$	1	0

Formally, let $V^i = \{w_1^i, w_2^i, \dots, w_{k_i}^i\}$ be the vocabulary of the corpus, let T^i be the collection of documents expressed in the language L^i, let $V^* = \bigcup_i V^i$ be the set of all the terms in all the languages, and let $k^* = |V^*|$ be the cardinality of this set. Let $\mathcal{D} = \{D_1, D_2, ..., D_d\}$ be the domain set. A MDM is fully defined by a $k^* \times k'$ matrix $\mathbf{D}$ representing in each cell $\mathbf{d_{i,z}}$ the *domain relevance* of the ith term of V^* with respect to the domain D_z.

As long as the similarity among texts in different languages has to be estimated, the information contained in the MDM is crucial. For example the two sentences *"I went to the hospital to make an HIV check"* and *"Ieri ho fatto il test dell'AIDS in clinica"* (lit. *yesterday I did the AIDS test in a clinic*) are very highly related, even if they share no tokens. Having "a priori" knowledge about the inter-lingual domain similarity among AIDS, HIV, hospital and clinica is then useful information to recognize inter-lingual topic similarity. Obviously this relation is less restrictive than a stronger association among translation pairs. In this chapter we will show that such a representation is sufficient to approach a Cross-language Text Categorization task, and can be easily acquired from comparable corpora.

6.2 Comparable Corpora

Comparable corpora are collections of texts in different languages regarding similar topics (e.g. a collection of news published by agencies in the same period). More restrictive requirements are expected for parallel corpora (i.e. corpora composed by texts which are mutual translations), while the class of multilingual corpora (i.e. collection of texts expressed in different languages without any additional requirement) is more general. Obviously parallel corpora are also comparable, while comparable corpora are also multilingual.

In a more precise way, let $L = \{L^1, L^2, \dots, L^l\}$ be a set of languages, let $T^i = \{t_1^i, t_2^i, \dots, t_n^i\}$ be a collection of texts expressed in the language $L^i \in L$, and let $\psi(t_h^j, t_z^i)$ be a function that returns 1 if t_z^i is the translation of

t_h^j and 0 otherwise. A *multilingual corpus* is the collection of texts defined by $T^* = \bigcup_i T^i$. If for every text $t_z^i \in T^i$ there exists one and only one text $t_h^j \in T^j$ such that the function $\psi(t_h^j, t_z^i)$ returns 1, we say that the corpora T^j and T^i are *parallel* (or *aligned* at document level). Two corpora are comparable when they are composed by texts about the same topics and produced in the same period (e.g. possibly from different news agencies), and it is not known if a function ψ exists, even if in principle it could exist and return 1 for a strict subset of document pairs.

There exist many interesting works about using parallel corpora for multilingual applications [63], such as Machine Translation [10], Cross-language Information Retrieval [53], and so on. However it is not always easy to find or build parallel corpora. This is the main reason because the "weaker" notion of comparable corpora is a matter of recent interest in the field of Computational Linguistics [27].

The texts inside comparable corpora, being about the same topics (i.e. about the same Semantic Domains), should refer to the same concepts by using different expressions in different languages. On the other hand, most of the proper nouns, relevant entities and words that have not yet been lexicalized, are expressed by using their original terms. As a consequence the *same entities* will be denoted with the *same words* in different languages, allowing to automatically detect couples of translation pairs just by looking at the word shape [48].

Our hypothesis is that comparable corpora contain a large amount of such words, just because texts referring to the same topics in different languages will often adopt the same terms to denote the same entities.[2] The presence of such common words in corpora allows us to induce second-order similarity relations for the other words in the lexicons by exploiting statistical techniques. In particular, we will demonstrate that the information provided by the analysis of the occurrences of such words is enough to induce a MDM (see Sect. 6.6).

In Sect. 6.6 we will show that multilingual domain information can be acquired from both parallel and comparable corpora. Even if, in principle, a better quality would be expected from parallel corpora, for practical reasons the second solution should be preferred because comparable corpora are more easily available than parallel ones.

6.3 The Cross-language Text Categorization Task

As fully discussed in Sect. 4.1, Text Categorization is the task of assigning category labels to documents. Categories are usually defined according to a variety of topics (e.g. SPORT, POLITICS, etc.) and, even if a large amount of

---

[2] According to our assumption, a possible additional criterion to decide whether two corpora are comparable is to estimate the percentage of terms in the intersection of their vocabularies.

hand tagged texts is required, the state-of-the-art supervised learning techniques represent a viable and well-performing solution for monolingual categorization problems.

On the other hand in the worldwide scenario of the WEB age, multilinguality is a crucial issue to deal with and to investigate, leading us to reformulate most of the classical NLP problems. In particular, monolingual Text Categorization can be reformulated as a *Cross-language Text Categorization* task, in which we have to cope with two or more languages (e.g. *English* and *Italian*). In this setting, the system is trained using labeled examples in a source language (e.g. *English*), and it classifies documents in a different target language (e.g. *Italian*).

Given that such a task has never been proposed in the literature, we defined a Cross-language Text Categorization task to perform our experiments. To this end, we used a news corpus kindly put at our disposal by *AdnKronos*, an important Italian news provider. The corpus consists of 32,354 Italian and 27,821 English news partitioned by AdnKronos in a number of four fixed categories: QUALITY_OF_LIFE, MADE_IN_ITALY, TOURISM, CULTURE_AND_SCHOOL. The English and the Italian corpora are comparable, in the sense stated in Sect. 6.2, i.e. they cover the same topics and the same period of time. Some news are translated in the other language (but *no* alignment indication is given), some others are present only in the English set, and some others only in the Italian. The average length of the news is about 300 words. We randomly split both the English and Italian part into 75% training and 25% test (see Table 6.2).

Table 6.2. Number of documents in the data set partitions

	English			Italian		
Categories	Training	Test	Total	Training	Test	Total
Quality_of_Life	5759	1989	7748	5781	1901	7682
Made_in_Italy	5711	1864	7575	6111	2068	8179
Tourism	5731	1857	7588	6090	2015	8105
Culture_and_School	3665	1245	4910	6284	2104	8388
Total	20866	6955	27821	24266	8088	32354

6.4 The Multilingual Vector Space Model

In Sect. 3.2 we introduced the Text VSM, a geometrical space in which the similarity among texts can be estimated by representing them by means of vectors having a dimension for each term in a controlled vocabulary. Unfortunately, such a model cannot be adopted in the multilingual settings, because the VSMs of different languages are mainly disjoint (i.e. the vocabularies of two different languages shares a few percentage of words). The similarity between two texts in different languages would often turn out zero. This situation is represented in Fig. 6.1, in which both the left-bottom and the right-upper regions of the matrix are totally filled by zeros.

A first attempt to solve this problem is to exploit the information provided by external knowledge sources, such as bilingual dictionaries, to collapse all the rows representing translation pairs. This situation is represented in Fig. 6.1 by the central region. The availability of a translation pairs repository allows us to define a Multilingual Text VSM, in which the dimensions of the two subspaces corresponding to each pair are collapsed. In the Multilingual Text VSM the similarity among texts in different languages can be estimated.

However, the main disadvantage of the Multilingual Text VSM is that it strongly relies on the availability of a multilingual lexical resource containing a list of translation pairs. For languages with scarce resources a bilingual dictionary may not be easily available. Secondly, an important requirement of such a resource is its coverage (i.e. the amount of possible translation pairs that are actually contained in it). Finally, another problem is that ambiguous terms could be translated in different ways, leading to collapsing together rows describing terms with very different meanings.

A similar operation can also be performed even if a bilingual lexical resource is not available under the assumption that the corpora in the two languages are comparable. In fact, the assumption of corpora comparability seen in Sect. 6.2, implies the presence of a number of common words, represented by the central rows of the matrix in Fig. 6.1. As illustrated in the previous section, it is reasonable to assume that most of these common words would refer to the same concepts, representing translation pairs. As far as comparable corpora are exploited, it is then possible to define a Multilingual Text VSM even if a bilingual dictionary is not available. Obviously, this model is rather poor because of its sparseness. In fact, the simple presence of these shared words is not enough to estimate the topic similarity between texts in different languages. In fact, even if the percentage of shared named entities in the vocabularies of the languages composing the comparable corpora is high, the frequency of these shared words is sensibly lower, because most of them are rare. The consequence is that most of the frequent terms in the two lexica will be represented by different dimensions even if they actually refer to the same concepts.

Similarly, in Sect. 3.2, we have also introduced a Term VSM, in which the similarity among terms is measured by representing them by means of vectors in a geometrical space having one dimension for each text in a monolingual corpus. As illustrated by Fig. 6.1, the Term VSM cannot be adopted to estimate the similarity among terms in different languages because the subspaces in which they are represented are totally disjoint. Thus, the Term VSM can be generalized to a Multilingual Term VSM only if a parallel corpus is available. In fact, parallel corpora are characterized by the existence of an alignment function ψ that allows us to collapse all the columns representing aligned texts, to define a Multilingual Term VSM where the similarity among terms in different languages can be computed. In the Multilingual Term VSM terms in different languages are then represented in the same space, having one dimension for each pair of aligned texts.

The same operation cannot be performed when only comparable corpora are used. In this cases it is not possible to compare the similarity between two terms in different languages in the Multilingual Term VSM. Unfortunately, the availability of parallel corpora is very limited, especially for languages with scarce resources.

		English texts					*Italian texts*				
		t_1^e	t_2^e	$\cdots$	t_{n-1}^e	t_n^e	t_1^i	t_2^i	$\cdots$	t_{m-1}^i	t_m^i
	w_1^e	0	1	$\cdots$	0	1	0	0	$\cdots$		
English Lexicon	w_2^e	1	1	$\cdots$	1	0	0	$\ddots$			
	$\vdots$	$\ldots$	$\ldots$	$\ldots$	$\ldots$	$\ldots$	$\vdots$		0		$\vdots$
	w_{p-1}^e	0	1	$\cdots$	0	0				$\ddots$	0
	w_p^e	0	1	$\cdots$	0	0			$\cdots$	0	0
common w_i	$w_1^{e/i}$	0	**1**	$\cdots$	0	0	0	0	$\cdots$	**1**	0
	$\vdots$	$\ldots$	$\ldots$	$\ldots$	$\ldots$	$\ldots$	$\ldots$	$\ldots$	$\ldots$	$\ldots$	$\ldots$
	w_1^i	0	0	$\cdots$			0	1	$\cdots$	1	1
Italian Lexicon	w_2^i	0	$\ddots$				1	1	$\cdots$	0	1
	$\vdots$	$\vdots$		0		$\vdots$	$\ldots$	$\ldots$	$\ldots$	$\ldots$	$\ldots$
	w_{q-1}^i				$\ddots$	0	0	1	$\cdots$	0	1
	w_q^i			$\cdots$	0	0	0	1	$\cdots$	1	0

Fig. 6.1. Multilingual term-by-document matrix

6.5 The Multilingual Domain Kernel

In this section we define the Multilingual Domain Kernel, a kernel function that can be exploited to estimate the topic similarity among two texts in different languages by taking into account the external knowledge provided by a MDM.

The Multilingual Domain Kernel relies on the definition of a Multilingual Domain Space, an extension of the Domain Space (see Sect. 3.3) in which both texts and terms in different languages are represent by means of Multilingual DVs, containing the degree of association between them and a common domain set. This representation allows a uniform comparison, avoiding the sparseness problem presented by both the Multilingual Term VSM and the Multilingual Text VSM.

As far as the text representation is concerned, the MDM $\mathbf{D}$ is used to define a function $\mathcal{D} : \mathbf{R}^{k^*} \rightarrow \mathbf{R}^{k'}$, that maps the document vectors $\mathbf{t}_j$ expressed in the Multilingual Text VSM into the vectors $\mathbf{t}'_j$ in the Multilingual Domain Space. The function $\mathcal{D}$ is defined by

$$\mathcal{D}(\mathbf{t}_j) = \mathbf{t}_j(\mathbf{I}^{\text{IDF}}\mathbf{D}) = \mathbf{t}'_j \quad (6.1)$$

where $\mathbf{I}^{\text{IDF}}$ is a diagonal matrix such that $i^{\text{IDF}}_{i,i} = \text{IDF}(w^l_i)$, $\mathbf{t}_j$ is represented as a row vector, and $\text{IDF}(w^l_i)$ is the *Inverse Document Frequency* of w^l_i evaluated in the corpus T^l.

In analogy to what was described in Sect. 3.7, it is also possible to extend the definition of the Multilingual Domain Kernel in order to estimate the similarity among terms in different languages. For brevity, we do not report here the exact mathematical definition of this operation. The Multilingual Domain Kernel is then specified by

$$K_{\text{D}}(t_i, t_j) = \frac{\langle \mathcal{D}(t_i), \mathcal{D}(t_j) \rangle}{\sqrt{\langle \mathcal{D}(t_j), \mathcal{D}(t_j) \rangle \langle \mathcal{D}(t_i), \mathcal{D}(t_i) \rangle}} \quad (6.2)$$

The MDM $\mathbf{D}$ can be determined in several ways, as for example by using hand-made lexical resources, such as WordNet Domains [56]. In the present work we followed the way to automatically acquire $\mathbf{D}$ from comparable corpora, exploiting the technique described in Sect. 6.6.

To evaluate the Multilingual Domain Kernel we compared it to a baseline kernel function, namely the BoW Kernel, that simply estimates the topic similarity in the Multilingual Text VSM, as described in Sect. 6.4. The BoW kernel is a particular case of the Domain Kernel, in which $\mathbf{D} = \mathbf{I}$, and $\mathbf{I}$ is the identity matrix.

6.6 Automatic Acquisition of Multilingual Domain Models

In Sect. 6.1 we introduced MDMs as a compact way to represent domain information in a multilingual scenario. In this section we will describe some methodology to acquire them from corpora. This operation can be performed in several ways, depending on the availability of multilingual lexical resources. In particular, we propose the use of Latent Semantic Analysis (LSA) [22] to induce a MDM, by generalizing the methodology introduced in Sect. 3.5 for the monolingual scenario.

In the monolingual settings, LSA is performed by means of a Singular Value Decomposition (SVD) of the term-by-document matrix **T** describing the corpus. In the multilingual settings, the SVD process can be performed on a multilingual term-by-document matrix describing a Multilingual VSM, in which some rows and/or columns corresponding to translating pairs and/or parallel texts have been collapsed, adopting the methodologies described in Sect. 6.4 to obtain Multilingual Term and Text VSMs. The collapsed rows/columns are used as "seeds" to start a statistical process that allows us to acquire the required second order relations among terms in different languages. It is then possible to define three different acquisition schemata for MDM, depending on the available lexical resources.

Acquisition from Parallel Corpora

In the literature [53] LSA has been used in multilingual settings to define a multilingual space, in which texts in different languages can be represented and compared. In that work, LSA strongly relied on the availability of aligned parallel corpora: texts in all the languages are represented in a term-by-document matrix (see Fig. 6.1) and then the columns corresponding to sets of translated documents are collapsed (i.e. they are replaced by their sum) before starting the LSA process. The effect of this step is to merge the subspaces (i.e. the right and the left sectors of the matrix in Fig. 6.1) in which the terms have been originally represented.

Acquisition from Bilingual Dictionaries

Another possibility is to collapse all the rows corresponding to translation pairs in a bilingual dictionary. The effect is to merge the subspaces (i.e. the upper and the bottom sectors of the matrix in Fig. 6.1) in which the texts have been originally represented. This operation is similar to that presented in [27].

Acquisition from Comparable Corpora

Comparable corpora can be used in all those cases in which neither an aligned parallel corpus nor a bilingual dictionary are available. In this case, the words in common to the vocabularies of the different languages can be exploited to obtain a set of translation pairs that can be used as "seeds" to start the SVD process. Of course, the higher the number of common words, the more information will be provided to the SVD algorithm to find common LSA dimensions for the two languages. As an example of the second-order similarity provided by acquiring MDMs from comparable corpora following the proposed approach, we can see in Table 6.3 the five most similar terms to the lemma *bank*. The similarity among terms is calculated by the cosine among the rows in the MDM, acquired from the data set used in our experiments (see Sect. 6.3). It is worth noting that the Italian lemma *banca* (i.e. bank in English) has a high similarity score to the English lemma *bank*. While this is not enough to have a precise term translation, it is sufficient to capture relevant aspects of topic similarity in a Cross-language Text Categorization task.

Table 6.3. Most similar terms to the English lemma *bank#n* in the MDM

Lemma#Pos	*Similarity Score*	*Language*
banking#n	0.96	Eng
credit#n	0.90	Eng
amro#n	0.89	Eng
unicredito#n	0.85	Ita
banca#n	0.83	Ita

In our experiments (see Sect. 6.7) we will restrict our attention to the acquisition from comparable corpora because we believe that this problem is the most interesting and the less well investigated.

6.7 Evaluation

In this chapter we proposed a novel approach to estimate the similarity among documents in different languages based on acquiring MDMs from comparable corpora in an unsupervised way, to define a Multilingual Domain Kernel, that can be used as a component of a supervised learning system to solve Multilingual Text Categorization problems. In this section we show the results obtained by adopting the Multilingual Domain Kernel in the Cross-language Text Categorization task defined in Sect. 6.3. In particular we tried both to train the system on the English data set and classify Italian documents and to train using Italian and classify the English test set. We compare the learning curves of the Multilingual Domain Kernel with the standard BoW Kernel, which is considered as a baseline for this task.

6.7.1 Implementation Details

In both the data sets we postagged the texts representing them by vectors containing the frequencies of each lemma with its part of speech. As a feature selection step, we considered only nouns, verbs, adjectives, and adverbs, removing all the remaining PoSs.

As a supervised learning device, we used the SVM implementation described in [40]. The Multilingual Domain Kernel is implemented by defining an explicit feature mapping as explained above, and by normalizing each vector. All the experiments have been performed with the standard SVM parameter settings.

We acquired a MDM by performing the SVD process on the term-by-document matrix representing the merged training partitions (i.e. English and Italian), and we considered only the first 400 dimensions.

6.7.2 Monolingual Text Categorization Results

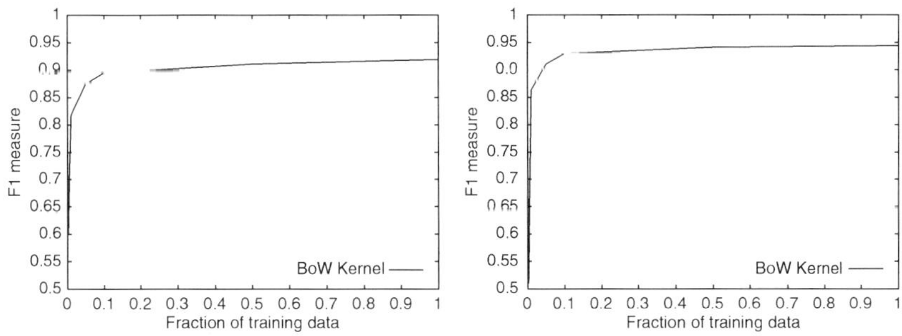

Fig. 6.2. Learning curves for the English (left) and the Italian (right) parts of the corpus

In order to define the upper bounds for the Cross-language Text Categorization task, we conducted two tests of classical monolingual Text Categorization by training and testing the system on Italian and English documents separately. For these tests we used the SVM with the BoW Kernel. Figure 6.2 reports the results.

6.7.3 Cross-language Text Categorization Results

As far as the Cross-language Text Categorization task is concerned, we tried the two possible options: we trained on the English part and we classified the Italian part, and we trained on the Italian and classified on the English part. The MDM was acquired running the SVD only on the joint (English and Italian) training parts.

Table 6.4 reports the vocabulary dimensions of the English and Italian training partitions, the vocabulary of the merged training, and how many common lemmata are present (about 14% of the total). Among the common lemmata, 97% are nouns and most of them are proper nouns. Thus the initial term-by-document matrix is a 43,384 × 45,132 matrix, while the MDM is represented by a 43,384 × 400 matrix. For this task we consider as a baseline the BoW Kernel.

Table 6.4. Number of lemmata in the training parts of the corpus

	# lemmata
English training	22,704
Italian training	26,404
English + Italian	43,384
common lemmata	5,724

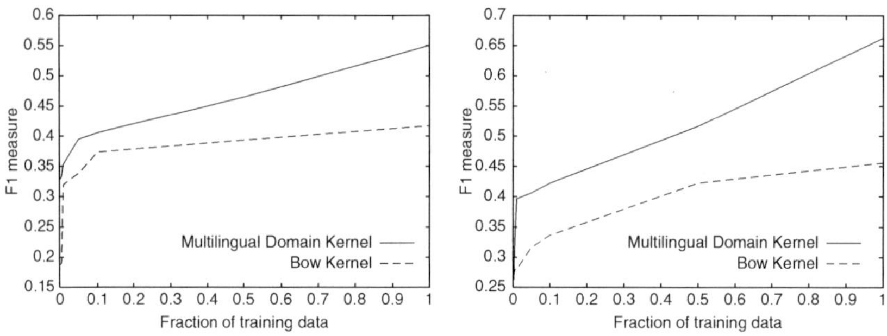

Fig. 6.3. Cross-language learning curves: training on Italian and test on English (right), training on English, test on Italian (left)

The results are reported in Fig. 6.3. Analyzing the learning curves, it is worth noting that when the quantity of training increases, the performance becomes better and better for the Multilingual Domain Kernel, suggesting that with more available training it could be possible to get closer to typical monolingual Text Categorization results.

6.8 Summary

In this chapter we proposed a solution to Cross-language Text Categorization based on acquiring MDMs from comparable corpora in a totally unsupervised way and without using any external knowledge source (e.g. bilingual dictionaries). These MDMs are exploited to define a generalized similarity function (i.e. the Multilingual Domain Kernel) among documents in different languages, which is used inside a SVM classification framework. The basis of the similarity function exploits the presence of common words to induce a second-order similarity for the other words in the lexicons. The results have shown that this technique is sufficient to capture relevant aspects of topic similarity in Cross-language Text Categorization tasks, obtaining substantial improvements over a simple baseline.

7

Conclusion and Perspectives for Future Research

7.1 Summary

In this book we summarized the more relevant results of five years of research on Semantic Domains in Computational Linguistics. As a linguistic work, we concentrated on studying the basic properties of Semantic Domains, a concept that we derived from the notion of Semantic Field, widely known in structural linguistics. We have shown that Semantic Domains are characterized by lexical coherence, a fundamental property that we corroborated by means of a corpus-based analysis. Lexical coherence is a key concept to understand the basics of the domain-driven approach to Natural Language Processing proposed here: it allows us to automatically induce Domain Models from corpora and to define the Domain-Driven Disambiguation methodology.

In addition, we remarked on the connections between lexical ambiguity and Semantic Domains, identifying a fundamental aspect of sense discrimination that we have called *domain polysemy*. Domain polysemy emerges when the same word frequently occurs in texts belonging to different domains. We also observed that Semantic Domains are shallow models for lexical variability: words belonging to the same domain denote very closely related concepts. For this reason Semantic Domains provide a precious knowledge source to estimate topic similarity among texts. Another very important property of Semantic Domains is their multilinguality. We have shown that the lexicon of different languages is structured into a common domain set that can be learned from comparable corpora in a totally unsupervised way.

After having provided a complete review of computational models for Semantic Domains, we introduced the notion of Domain Model. Domain Models are represented by matrices describing the associations among words and a domain set. Domain Models represent ambiguity and variability, and can be profitably used to estimate the domain relevance for texts and terms. We have shown that Domain Models can be induced from corpora in a totally unsupervised way, and then exploited to represent texts in a Domain Space, where topic similarity is better estimated. In addition we proposed a multilingual

DOI: 10.1007/978-3-540-68158-8_7,

extension for Domain Models, namely Multilingual Domain Models, and we presented a novel unsupervised technique to induce them from comparable corpora.

To support our claims we performed a set of task-based evaluations, motivating this approach by a "meaning-is-use" assumption. We believe that theories for lexical semantics cannot be sustained by means of speaker judgments only, because they are subjective and artificial. On the contrary, we think that meaning emerges from the concrete situations where the expressions are formulated, and cannot be studied in isolation as a domain-independent notion. Thus we did an indirect evaluation of our linguistic claims, performed by evaluating the improvements due to the use of Domain Models into a set of different Natural Language Processing tasks. The basic assumption of our task-based evaluation is that if the same computational model improves the performance of systems in different tasks, such as Text Categorization and Word Sense Disambiguation, the underlying linguistic phenomena involved in those tasks are correctly captured and modeled. The consistent and substantial improvements over the state-of-the-art approaches that we obtained across different languages and application domains demonstrate the correctness of our linguistic claims about Semantic Domains.

As far as evaluation is concerned, this work can then be regarded as a Natural Language Processing study. In particular we applied domain-driven technologies to three different tasks: Text Categorization, Word Sense Disambiguation and Cross-language Text Categorization. The main results we obtained in Text Categorization are to design a semi-supervised learning schema that allowed us to reduce drastically the amount of labeled training data required for learning. This feature opens new perspectives for the definition of minimally supervised Text Categorization systems, to be exploited for user modeling and other application scenarios where it is difficult to provide huge amounts of labeled training data. In addition, we proposed an Intensional Learning schema for Text Categorization, consisting of describing the categories by means of lists of relevant terms instead of labeled texts. The duality of the domain-based representations allowed us to perform this task by just using the category name to describe each class, achieving performances close to human agreement.

The most impressive results we obtained were achieved in the Word Sense Disambiguation task. We were able to design a semi-supervised learning strategy, consisting of acquiring Domain Models from a large set of untagged examples of the word to be disambiguated, and then applying them to define semi-supervised Word Sense Disambiguation systems. Using the domain-driven approach, we surpassed the state-of-the-art while reducing substantially the amount of labeled data required for learning. In addition we defined the Domain-Driven Disambiguation methodology, an unsupervised approach to Word Sense Disambiguation that relies on domain information only. We applied this methodology to an all-words task, reporting the state-of-the-art result for unsupervised systems. In addition, the coarse-grained sense distinctions reported in WordNet Domains allowed us to achieve high performance in the easier task to solve domain ambiguity, by adopting the unsupervised Domain-Driven Disambiguation approach. We believe that domain-grained sense distinctions can be profitably used by all those applications that do not require finer grained sense distinctions, such as Information Retrieval.

Finally, we evaluated Multilingual Domain Models on a Cross-language Text Categorization task. Multilingual Domain Models were acquired from comparable corpora in a totally unsupervised way, and then exploited to define a Multilingual Domain Space, where texts in different languages can be represented and compared. The obtained multilingual representations were used to develop a Cross-language Text Categorization system. Multilingual Domain Models allowed us to achieve significant improvements over a baseline approach based on Bag-of-Words, demonstrating the effectiveness of the lexical representations so acquired and supporting the multilingual assumption we put forward about Semantic Domains.

7.2 Future Work

The concept of Semantic Domain we provided in this book is an attempt to clarify the notion of Semantic Field in Computational Linguistics, and provides many interesting insights and empirical observations that can be used as a basis for further investigations. First of all, it would be necessary to investigate in a more detailed way many directions that have not been fully explored in this work, due to our time constraints. Secondly, it would be interesting to apply domain-driven technologies to concrete application scenarios. Finally, we believe that the research presented here is just a small step forward in the empirical investigations on the idea of the Semantic Fields, and much more work can be done in this direction. Our future research will concentrate on providing a richer internal structure to the lexicon of each field, by identifying paradigmatic relations among entities and concepts in each domain. Hence our future work will be about Ontology Learning.

7.2.1 Consolidation of the Present Work

Many experiments have to be done to fully understand the basics of our approach. First of all, it would be necessary to better investigate the problem of choosing the right dimensionality of the domain set for a particular task. To this end, both a theoretical and an empirical investigation would be required. From a theoretical point of view, a better clarification of the properties characterizing lexical coherence is crucial to define a discrimination criterion for Semantic Domains. Empirically, the performance of the domain-driven systems could be analyzed by varying the dimensionality of the domain set.

The Domain Space can also be exploited in Information Retrieval. In particular we believe that such a representation would improve substantially recall when applied to small collections of documents, such as the archive of a company or the user's personal documents. In fact, traditional Information Retrieval methods, based on bags-of-words, rely on a redundancy assumption that can be only presupposed in Web scale collections, while in smaller collections their performances are substantially penalized by the lack of variability. We believe that the information provided by the Domain Models could help Information Retrieval systems to improve recall on such small collections, because variability can be taken into account.

In our experiments, we used a term clustering methodology based on Latent Semantic Analysis to acquire our Domain Models. Different clustering techniques can also be explored and compared for unsupervised learning of Domain Models. For example, different feature indexing methods can be designed to take into account paradigmatic aspects. Nouns could be indexed by their modifiers or by the predicates of which they are objects or subjects, defining a feature representation similar to those adopted by Porzig (see Sect. 2.1). Another relevant aspect of this research, not considered yet, is to provide an explicit evaluation of the quality of the acquired Domain Models, for example by comparing them to the term clusters in WordNet Domains.

Our methodology for Word Sense Disambiguation can also be improved in several ways. An interesting direction is to integrate syntactic information into our kernel combination schema. For the future we plan to integrate full parsing by including a TreeKernel (i.e. a kernel function to estimate the similarity among parse trees, see Appendix A.6) into our kernel combination schema. In addition, we are going to evaluate this methodology in an all-words task, where just minimal supervision is available.

Finally, we are going to improve our multilingual acquisition technique in several ways. Our basic assumption is that named entities are expressed by the same terms in different languages. In our experiments we only identified common lemmata, we did not exploit named entity recognition systems. We plan to perform this analysis in future experiments. In addition, we are improving the matching methodology by adopting string similarity measures (e.g. String Kernels) to detect a higher number of candidate translation pairs. Another interesting experiment that we did not perform because of time constraints is to compare the results of the acquisition methodology from comparable corpora to some acquisition technique based on parallel corpora, in order to define an upper bound for the Cross-language Text Categorization task. Multilingual Domain Models can also be applied to Cross-language Information Retrieval, for example selecting dynamically sub-portions of bilingual lexical resources describing the domain of the terms in the queries.

7.2.2 Domain-Driven Technologies

The research proposed here opens new perspectives to develop a wide range of Natural Language Processing systems to be used in real application scenarios. From this point of view, the most useful feature of the domain-driven technology is the possibility of reducing the amount of labeled training data.

In a wide variety of tasks, it is practically impossible to collect large sets of labeled examples for the categories required by the application domain. Minimally supervised systems offer a great advantage in developing content-based techniques for user modeling. For example mail clients could be provided by automatic mail categorization procedures that can be initialized by the user, just providing a few documents. The user's interests could also be recognized by analyzing the Domain Models acquired from their own documents. Domain-driven user modeling techniques seem suitable for text summarization, segmentation and for many other tasks that should be modeled dynamically according to the user's requirements.

Even if the results are not reported in this work, we have also participated in several projects by applying Domain Models to different application scenarios, as for example e-learning and bioinformatics. We developed a module of a general system for the automatic assessment of student's free text answers [73], reporting substantial improvements due to a domain-driven analysis of the answer's content. In the Bio-NLP field, we estimated gene-protein similarity by acquiring Domain Models from the biomedical scientific literature.

Another set of usages we have in mind for our domain-driven technologies is related to the knowledge management area. Systems for automatic archiving and retrieval would benefit from domain-driven Text Categorization systems, and the Intensional Learning approach could be used to populate the nodes of existing ontologies with related texts. In addition the Domain Models obtained from unsupervised learning can be used as a basis to initiate a domain-specific ontology learning processes, while Term Categorization techniques can be exploited for pruning, tuning and populating existing lexical resources, such as WordNet.

7.3 Conclusion

It is premature to draw a definitive conclusion for the research on Semantic Domains, and a huge amount of work has to be done. We hope that other researchers in the community will take advantage of our work and we believe that the industrial development of the technologies described here will lead to the implementation of more user-friendly applications.

From our side, we are going further with the work on Semantic Fields in Computational Linguistics, by following the research direction of implementing computational models to support and corroborate linguistic theories. We will concentrate on providing an internal structure of paradigmatic relations to the concepts of each field. To this end, we are going to acquire Domain Models from a Web-scale corpus and then analyze the relations among the terms in each domain. Relations among terms will be automatically inferred from the syntagmatic associations they establish with verbs and adjectives, analyzed from the corresponding domain-specific text collections. Relations can be represented by binary predicates of the form $P(E_1, E_2)$ where P is a verb and both E_1 and E_2 are terms or entities belonging to the same domain. The result of this further analysis is then a set of domain-specific ontologies, describing the relations among the domain-specific entities we have found in the corpus, and their conceptualization. These ontologies are then Semantic Fields in Trier's sense, i.e. sets of highly paradigmatically related terms.

A

Appendix: Kernel Methods for Natural Language Processing

This appendix is about Kernel Methods, the learning framework in which we designed several experiments described in this book. Kernel Methods are instance-based learning algorithms that exploit kernel functions to estimate the similarity among objects in the instance space. Even if the class of Kernel Methods includes a large set of algorithms for a wide variety of Machine Learning tasks, such as clustering [6], regression [91], and one class learning [60], in this appendix we will focus our attention on binary classification learning problems only.

The first sections of this brief overview are about the problem of learning by risk minimization. In this part we describe a class of learning algorithms, namely linear classifiers, that can be trained by means of both feature and instance-based learning schemata. The notation adopted there is mainly based on the introduction to Kernel Methods provided by [39].

In the second part of this appendix we will describe a set of kernel functions that can be profitably used to design NLP algorithms. In particular, we illustrate a set of kernels to model the similarity among the basic linguistic objects involved in most of the NLP problems: text, sequences and trees. In this part we will mainly refer to the comprehensive overview provided by [81].

A.1 Supervised Learning

The *classification learning* problem is to find the unknown *classification function* $f : \mathcal{X} \rightarrow \mathcal{P}(Y)$[1] that maps *objects* $x \in X$ into a finite set of *categories* $y \in Y$ basely solely on a *training sample* of labeled objects $\mathbf{z} = (\mathbf{x}, \mathbf{y}) = ((x_1, y_1), ..., (x_m, y_m)) \subseteq (\mathcal{X} \times Y)$ drawn from an unknown distribution $\mathbf{P}_{\mathcal{X}Y}$. If the category set is composed by only two classes (i.e. $Y = \{-1, +1\}$) we say that the learned categorization function is a *binary classifier*. In general, any *multiclass* classification problem (i.e. a problem

[1] $\mathcal{P}(Y)$ is the set of all the possible subsets of Y, i.e. the *power set*.

in which $n > 2$ categories have to be discriminated) can be approached by defining $n-1$ different binary classifiers and by selecting the most confident prediction according to a voting strategy. In the rest of this appendix we will focus on binary classification problems only.

The goal of any learning algorithm is to select the best categorization function f^* from a *hypothesis space* $\mathcal{F} \subseteq \{-1,+1\}^{\mathcal{X}}$ (i.e. the set of all the possible categorization hypothesis that can be formulated by the particular learning algorithm). The size of the hypothesis space actually explored by the learning algorithm is determined by its *bias* (i.e. the additional assumptions exploited by the learning algorithm to estimate the categorization function).

In many cases, a learning algorithm is characterized as an *optimization problem*, consisting of selecting the hypothesis $f^* \in \mathcal{F}$ that satisfies a specific optimization criterion. A very common optimization criterion is the *risk minimization* principle, defined as follows:

$$f^* = \arg\min_{f \in \mathcal{F}} R[f] \tag{A.1}$$

where $R[f] = \mathbf{E}_{\mathcal{X},Y}[l(f(\mathcal{X}), Y)]$ is called the *expected risk*, $l : \mathbb{R} \times Y \to \mathbb{R}$ is a risk function that measure how costly it is when the prediction for x is $f(x)$ but the true class is y, e.g. the *zero-one risk* $l_{0-1} : \mathbb{R} \times Y \to \mathbb{R}$ defined by

$$l_{0-1}(f(x), y) = \mathbf{1}_{yf(x) \leqslant 0} \tag{A.2}$$

returning 1 if x is correctly classified (i.e. $\text{sign}(f(x)) = \text{sign}(y)$), 0 otherwise. The lower the expected risk, the more accurate the classification function.

Given the available training data $\mathbf{z}$, the "true" expected risk $\mathbf{E}_{\mathcal{X},Y}[l(f(\mathcal{X}), Y)]$ cannot be estimated exactly, because the distribution $\mathbf{P}_{\mathcal{X}Y}$ is unknown. On the other hand, according to sampling theory, the higher $|\mathbf{z}|$, the closer the distributions $\mathbf{P}_{\mathbf{z}}$ and $\mathbf{P}_{\mathcal{X}Y}$. As an approximation, the expected risk can be estimated by the *empirical risk*, defined by

$$R_{\text{emp}}[f, \mathbf{z}] = \frac{1}{m} \sum_{i=1}^{m} l(f(x_i), y_i) \tag{A.3}$$

Minimizing the empirical risk is not a good optimization criterion, because it could cause the learning algorithm to overfit the training sample (i.e. the empirical risk is sensibly lower than the "true" expected risk, leading to false predictions over unseen data). *Overfitting* is strongly related to the *bias* of the learning algorithm, and depends on the function class adopted to formulate the categorization hypothesis. A function class $\mathbf{f} = \{f_\alpha | \alpha \in \mathbb{R}^k\}$ is a family of functions whose members are determined by specifying a set of parameters α (e.g. linear functions, quadratic functions). Very expressive hypothesis spaces could lead the algorithm to overfit the training examples. In order to avoid overfitting, it is necessary to impose an additional constraint to the optimization function, i.e. a regularizer $\Omega : \mathcal{F} \to \mathbb{R}^+$. The expected risk is then estimated as follows:

$$R[f] = R_{\text{emp}}[f, \mathbf{z}] + \lambda \Omega[\mathbf{f}] \tag{A.4}$$

The regularizer Ω can be thought of as a penalization term for the "expressivity" of the hypothesis space explored by of particular learning algorithm: a simple function that explains most of the data is preferable to a complex one.[2]

A specific way to control the expressivity of the hypothesis space is provided the Vapnik-Chervonenkis (VC) theory [90]. According to this theory, with probability $1 - \delta$, the upper bound for the estimation of the expected risk is provided by

$$\mathbf{E}_{\mathcal{X},Y}[l(f(\mathcal{X}), Y)] \leqslant R_{\text{emp}}[f, \mathbf{z}] + \sqrt{\frac{h(\log \frac{2m}{h} + 1) - \ln \frac{\delta}{4}}{m}} \tag{A.5}$$

where and $h = VC(\mathbf{f})$ is the VC dimension of the function class $\mathbf{f}$ explored by the learning algorithm. The second addend of the right term of Eq. A.5 can be exploited to define a regularizer Ω, to be substituted in Eq. A.4, obtaining the principle of *Structural Risk Minimization* [90]. According to this principle, function classes having a lower VC dimension should be preferred to more complex ones, because they prevent the risk of overfitting.

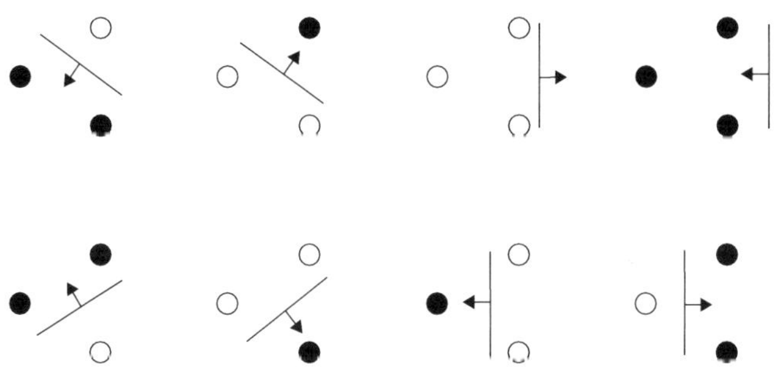

Fig. A.1. Three points in a bidimensional space can be shattered by a straight line regardless of the particular category assignment

The VC dimension $h = VC(\mathbf{f})$ of a function class $\mathbf{f}$ is the maximum number of points that can be shattered by it. A class of functions $\mathbf{f}$ is said to shatter the set of instances $\mathbf{x}'$ if, for any of the $2^{|\mathbf{x}'|}$ possible category assignments $\mathbf{z}' = (\mathbf{x}', \mathbf{y}')$, there exists a function $f_\alpha \in \mathbf{f}$ such that $R_{\text{emp}}[f_\alpha, \mathbf{z}'] = 0$, i.e. the function is able to separate the positive from the negative examples without exceptions. The higher the VC dimension of the function class explored by the classifier, the higher its risk of overfitting. For example, it is possible to

[2] This principle is a machine learning interpretation of the very well known Occam's Razor: when multiple explanations are available for a phenomenon, the simplest version is preferred.

shatter $n+1$ points represented in a n-dimensional space by means of an hyperplane, as illustrated by Fig. A.1. On the other hand, the class of the sinusoids in a bidimensional space (i.e. $f(x) = \text{sign}(\theta \sin(\omega x))$) has unlimited VC dimension [9].

A.2 Feature-Based vs. Instance-Based Learning

A key concept in supervised learning is the distinction between feature and instance-based learning. Feature-based learning algorithms represent the objects by means of feature vectors while instance-based learning algorithms rely on the definition of a similarity metric $K : \mathcal{X} \times \mathcal{X} \rightarrow \mathbb{R}$ among the objects in the instance space. It reflects in the two different learning paradigms defined below.

Feature-based Learning

Feature-based classifiers represent the objects by means of feature vectors. A feature is a function $\phi_i : \mathcal{X} \rightarrow \mathbb{R}$ that maps each object $x \in \mathcal{X}$ to a real value $\phi_i(x)$. Combining n features $\phi_1(x), \ldots, \phi_n(x)$ results in a feature mapping $\phi : \mathcal{X} \rightarrow \mathbb{R}^n = \mathcal{K}$ such that $\phi(x) = \mathbf{x} \in \mathbb{R}^n$ and the space $\mathcal{K}$ is called a *feature space*. In general, the wider the feature space, the larger the hypothesis space determined by the learning algorithm. The categorization function formulated by a feature-based classifier belongs to the following categorization schema:

$$f(x) = g(\phi_1(x), \ldots, \phi_n(x)) \tag{A.6}$$

Applying feature-based classifiers to concrete domains consists mainly on defining appropriate feature extraction techniques for the objects to be represented.

Instance-based Learning

As an alternative, instance-based classifiers rely on a similarity metric $K : \mathcal{X} \times \mathcal{X} \rightarrow \mathbb{R}$ among objects $x \in \mathcal{X}$ and do not require, at least in principle, the definition of any explicit feature extraction algorithm. The categorization function formulated by an instance-based learning algorithm belongs to the following categorization schema:

$$f(x) = g(K(x_1, x), \ldots, K(x_m, x)) \tag{A.7}$$

Applying instance-based classifiers to concrete domains consists mainly on defining appropriate similarity metrics for the objects to be compared.

A typical similarity function, exploited by most of the instance-based learning algorithms, is the dot product among feature vectors (i.e. $\text{sim}(x_i, x_j) = \langle \mathbf{x_i}, \mathbf{x_j} \rangle$). In many other cases, it is possible to define similarity metrics working directly in the instance space, in order to avoid any explicit feature mapping. For example, the similarity among trees or sequences can be estimated by recursively counting the number of common substructures, allowing a fast exploration of a huge hypothesis space in a very efficient way.

A.3 Linear Classifiers

Linear classifiers are supervised learning algorithms characterized by the following function class:

$$f_{\mathbf{w}}(x) = \langle \mathbf{x}, \mathbf{w} \rangle + b \tag{A.8}$$

where $\mathbf{x} = \Phi(x)$ and $\mathbf{w} \in \mathcal{W} = \mathbb{R}^n$ is a n-dimensional vector.

From a geometrical point of view, linear classifiers separate the feature space into two open half spaces by means of hyperplanes, as illustrated by Fig. A.2. The decision surface of a linear classifier is determined by

$$\tilde{X}(\mathbf{w}) = \{\mathbf{x} \in \mathcal{K} | \langle \mathbf{x}, \mathbf{w} \rangle + b = 0\} \tag{A.9}$$

To simplify the notation, we can also restrict the hypothesis space to all those hyperplanes passing through the origin of the feature space:

$$f_{\mathbf{w}}(x) = \langle \mathbf{x}, \mathbf{w} \rangle \tag{A.10}$$

It can be shown that the classification functions provided by classifiers defined according to Eq. A.10 are very close to those provided by Eq. A.8, especially when high dimensional feature spaces are explored, as for most of the NLP problems. Will adopt Eq. A.10 in the rest of this appendix, following the presentation provided by [39].

The goal of any learning algorithm for linear classifiers is to select the vector $\mathbf{w}^*$ whose associated categorization function $f_{\mathbf{w}^*}$ minimizes the expected risk. Geometrical considerations allow us to reformulate this learning problem in terms of separability among instances in a feature space. To this end we introduce the concept of functional margin. The *functional margin* $\tilde{\gamma}_i(\mathbf{w})$ of an example $x \in \mathcal{X}$ measures the distance between the example and the decision surface, i.e. $\tilde{\gamma}_i(\mathbf{w}) = y_i \langle \mathbf{x}_i, \mathbf{w} \rangle$, as illustrated by Fig. A.2. The functional margin of an example is positive when the categorization function determined by the hyperplane correctly predicts its class. The functional margin $\tilde{\gamma}_{\mathbf{z}}(\mathbf{w})$ of an hyperplane is the minimum functional margin for all the objects in the training sample, defined by

$$\tilde{\gamma}_{\mathbf{z}}(\mathbf{w}) = \min_{(x_i, y_i) \in \mathbf{z}} y_i \langle \mathbf{x}_i, \mathbf{w} \rangle \tag{A.11}$$

The functional margin of a hyperplane $\mathbf{w}$ on the training sample $\mathbf{z}$ is positive if and only if $R_{\mathrm{emp}}[f_{\mathbf{w}}, \mathbf{z}] = 0$, i.e. no wrong predictions are committed.[3] In this case, we say that the sample set $\mathbf{z}$ is *linearly separable* in the feature space.

[3] Sometimes it is more convenient to estimate the *geometrical margin* $\gamma_{\mathbf{z}}(\mathbf{w})$ as the ratio between the functional margin and the norm of the vector $\mathbf{w}$, defined by:

$$\gamma_{\mathbf{z}}(\mathbf{w}) = \frac{\tilde{\gamma}_{\mathbf{z}}(\mathbf{w})}{\|\mathbf{w}\|} \tag{A.12}$$

The Primal Perceptron Algorithm

The *Primal Perceptron* algorithm is an iterative procedure that can be used to train linear classifiers. As already introduced, any linear classifier is fully determined by the vector $\mathbf{w}$. The perceptron algorithm estimates this vector as follows:

1. Set the vector $\mathbf{w}$ to the null vector $\mathbf{0}$.
2. For each $(x_i, y_i) \in \mathbf{z}$, update the vector $\mathbf{w}$ to $\mathbf{w} + y_i\mathbf{x_i}$ if $y_i\langle \mathbf{x}_i, \mathbf{w}\rangle < 0$ (i.e. the example x_i is not correctly categorized by the function $f_{\mathbf{w}}$).
3. If $R_{\text{emp}}[f_{\mathbf{w}}, \mathbf{z}] = 0$ (i.e. no mistake occurs during an iteration of step 2) then stop, else reiterate step 2.

If the training sample is linearly separable, the primal perceptron algorithm converges to a consistent hypothesis in a finite number of steps, as demonstrated by the *Perceptron Convergence Theorem*. Let ζ be the radius of the smallest hypersphere enclosing all the training objects represented in the feature space. If the training sample is linearly separable the number of cycles required by the perceptron learning algorithm to converge is bounded by:[4]

$$\left(\frac{\zeta}{\gamma_{\mathbf{z}}(\mathbf{w}^*)}\right)^2 \tag{A.13}$$

The main limitations of this algorithm can be summarized as follows:

1. The solution $\mathbf{w}^*$ is *not unique*. As illustrated by Fig. A.2, there exist many different hyperplanes separating the same sample set, some of them generalizing better than others. The perceptron algorithm is not able to distinguish among them.
2. It is *not robust*: the training sample should be linearly separable in order to reach a solution and the presence of outliers in the training data would lead it to converge very slowly.

Support Vector Machines

In this section we describe Support Vector Machines (SVM), a very well known class of instance-based learning algorithms that can be used to train linear classifiers. SVMs are the state-of-the-art framework for supervised learning.

The SVM algorithm solves the two main problems affecting the perceptron learning algorithm already discussed. To solve (1) it imposes a regularizer to the optimization function allowing to select a (unique) *maximal margin hyperplane*. To solve (2), it introduces *soft margins* by adopting a cost function that assigns positive weights to the misclassified examples, according to their distance from the hyperplane. In the next two subparagraphs we will describe and motivate these particular choices.

[4] This theorem suggests that the higher the geometrical margin of the separating hyperplane, the better the learning performances.

Maximal Margin Hyperplanes

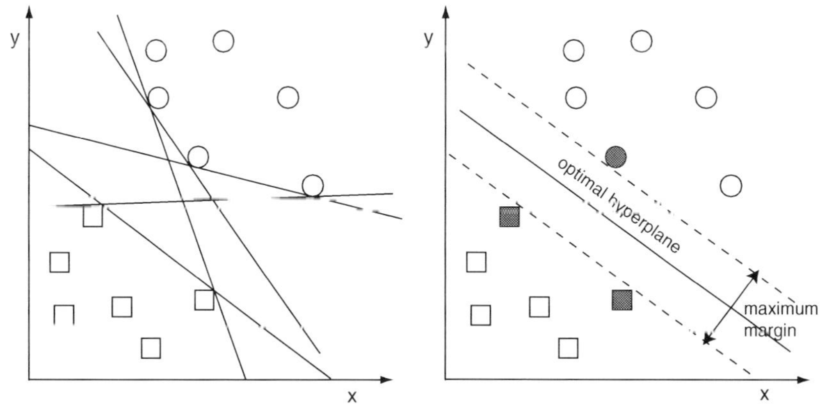

Fig. A.2. Maximal margin hyperplane

Equation A.13 shows that the number of steps required by the perceptron algorithm to converge is related to the geometrical margin of the estimated separating hyperplane, motivating the assumption that the hyperplane having maximal margin (i.e. the hyperplane associated to $\mathbf{w}^* \in W$ such that the geometrical margin $\gamma_{\mathbf{z}}(\mathbf{w}^*)$ is maximized) should be selected to improve generalization. This condition allows the SVM algorithm to find a unique solution $\mathbf{w}^*$ for any linearly separable sample set $\mathbf{z}$, as geometrically illustrated in Fig. A.2, leading to the formulation of the following optimization criterion:

$$\mathbf{w}^* = \text{argmax}_{\mathbf{w} \in \mathcal{W}} \frac{\tilde{\gamma}_{\mathbf{z}}(\mathbf{w})}{||\mathbf{w}||} \tag{A.14}$$

Without loss of generality, we can restrict the hypothesis space to the hyperplanes having unitary functional margin $\mathcal{W}(\mathbf{z}) = \{\mathbf{w} \in \mathcal{W} | \tilde{\gamma}_{\mathbf{z}}(\mathbf{w}) = 1\}$. Following this assumption the maximal margin hyperplane is determined by the vector $\mathbf{w} \in \mathcal{W}(\mathbf{z})$ of minimal norm. The optimization functions becomes

$$\text{minimize } ||\mathbf{w}||^2 \tag{A.15}$$
$$\text{subject to } y_i \langle \mathbf{x}_i, \mathbf{w} \rangle \geqslant 1 \; i = 1, \ldots, m \tag{A.16}$$
$$\mathbf{w} \in \mathcal{W}(\mathbf{z}) \tag{A.17}$$

where the constraints guarantee that $\mathbf{w}^*$ actually separates the positive from the negative objects in the training sample. This optimization function is adopted by *hard margin SVMs*, so called because they do not allow misclassification in the training sample.

Soft margins. To ensure convergence on non-linearly separable sample sets it is necessary to allow misclassifications on the training sample. This operation can be done by relaxing the constraint defined in Eq. A.15. To this end we modify the loss function, in order to assign a different risk to each misclassified example, depending on its distance from the separating hyperplane. The *soft margin SVM* algorithm exploits the following loss function to estimate the empirical error:

$$l_{\text{soft}}(f_{\mathbf{w}}(x), y) = \max[1 - y_i\langle \mathbf{w}, \mathbf{x}_i\rangle, 0] = \xi_i \tag{A.18}$$

The *slack variables* ξ_i associated to the outliers of the classification regions identified by $\mathbf{w}$ have non null positive values, while those associated to correctly classified instances are zero, as illustrated in Fig. A.3.

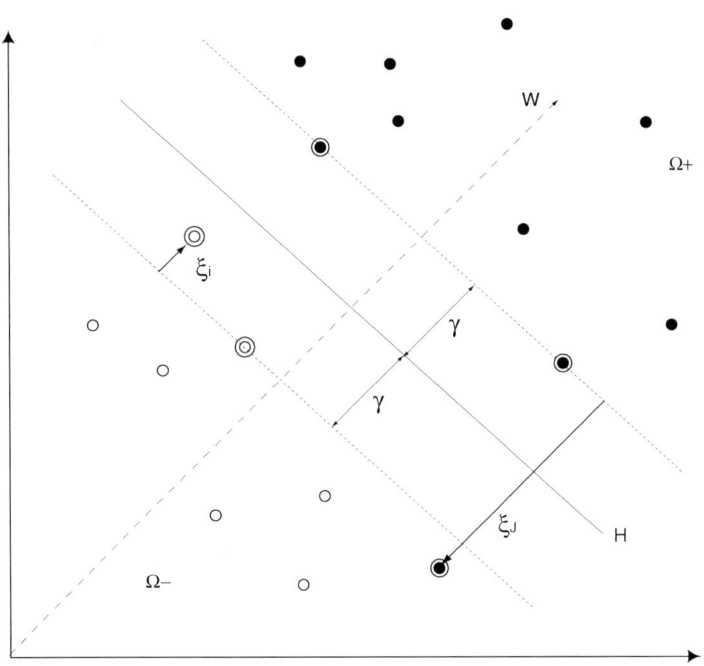

Fig. A.3. Soft margin

The goal of the SVM algorithm is to minimize the empirical risk, estimated by means of the cost function described above (i.e. $R_{\text{emp}}[f_{\mathbf{w}}, \mathbf{z}] = \frac{1}{m}\sum_{i=1}^{m} \xi_i$), while maximizing the margin. To this end, the following optimization criterion is defined:

$$\text{minimize} \sum_{i=1}^{m} \xi_i + Cm\|\mathbf{w}\|^2 \tag{A.19}$$

$$\text{subject to } y_i \langle \mathbf{x}_i, \mathbf{w} \rangle \geqslant 1 - \xi_i \ , \ \xi_i \geqslant 0, \ i = 1, \dots, m \tag{A.20}$$

$$\mathbf{w} \in \mathcal{W}(\mathbf{z}) \tag{A.21}$$

The parameter C regulates the tradeoff between the empirical risk and the complexity term. If $C = 0$, the SVM algorithm works with a hard margin, because the algorithm converges to the solution having minimal empirical error, as for the hard margin case. For higher values of C, hyperplanes having higher margins will be preferred, with the effect of increasing the empirical error to allow misclassifications, while reducing the risk of overfitting. In practical applications it is not clear how to set this parameter; then it is frequently optimized by adopting cross-validation techniques.

A.4 Kernel Methods

As introduced in Sect. A.2, instance-based learning algorithms rely on the definition of a similarity metric among the instances to be classified, and do not require any explicit feature mapping. In this section we introduce a particular class of instance-based classifiers, namely Kernel Methods, that allows an instance-based solution for the problem of estimating the best separating hyperplane required to train a linear classifier.

Linear classifiers are inherently feature-based, because separating hyperplanes are implicitly defined in feature spaces. On the other hand, any feature space can be explored indirectly by defining instance-based algorithms working in the instance space. In fact, linear classifiers have a (dual) instance-based formulation that relies on the definition of kernel functions, i.e. similarity functions among objects in the instance space.

To show this we notice that any solution $\mathbf{w}$ provided by the primal perceptron algorithm (see Sect. A.3), is obtained updating the vector $\mathbf{w_o}$ by summing the feature vectors $\mathbf{x} = \mathbf{\Phi}(x)$ of all the misclassified examples. The best separating hyperplane is then estimated by a linear combination of the feature vectors describing the training instances:

$$\mathbf{w} = \sum_{i=1}^{m} \alpha_i \mathbf{x}_i \tag{A.22}$$

Substituting the previous formula in Eq. A.10, we define a linear classifier that relies only on the similarities among objects, estimated by a kernel function in the (dual) instance space.

$$\begin{aligned} f_{\mathbf{w}}(x) &= \langle \mathbf{x}, \mathbf{w} \rangle = \langle \mathbf{x}, \sum_{i=1}^{m} \alpha_i \mathbf{x}_i \rangle \\ &= \sum_{i=1}^{m} \alpha_i \langle \mathbf{x}, \mathbf{x}_i \rangle = \sum_{i=1}^{m} \alpha_i K(x, x_i) = f_{\alpha}(x) \end{aligned} \tag{A.23}$$

where $K(x_i, x_j) \stackrel{\text{def}}{=} \langle \mathbf{\Phi}(x_i), \mathbf{\Phi}(x_j) \rangle$ is a kernel function.[5] In the dual formulation, the function class characterizing a linear classifier is then defined as follows:

$$f_\alpha(x) = \sum_{i=1}^{m} \alpha_i K(x_i, x) \tag{A.24}$$

Instance-based learning algorithms exploiting kernel functions are also known as *Kernel Methods*. The basic idea behind Kernel Methods is to embed the data into a suitable feature space $\mathcal{K}$ via a mapping function $\mathbf{\Phi} : \mathcal{X} \rightarrow \mathcal{K}$, and then use a linear algorithm for discovering nonlinear patterns. Kernel Methods allow us to build a modular system, as the kernel function acts as an interface between the data and the learning algorithm. Thus the kernel function becomes the only domain specific module of the system, while the learning algorithm is a general purpose component. Potentially a kernel function can work with any kernel-based algorithm, such as for example SVM.

In the following paragraphs we will provide dual formulations for the two learning algorithms described in the previous section. In the dual space, only the similarities among objects are taken into account, leading to the definition of instance-based learning algorithms.

The Kernel Perceptron Algorithm

In analogy to the Primal Perceptron, illustrated in Sect. A.3, the Kernel Perceptron algorithm adopts a zero-one loss function and does not exploit any regularizer. The training is performed by initializing α to the null vector (i.e. $\alpha = \mathbf{0}$) at the first step, and, for each instance in the sample set, by updating the jth weight α_j, assigned to the example $x_j \in \mathbf{x}$, to the new value $\alpha_j + y_j f_\alpha(\mathbf{x}_j)$ if $y_j f_\alpha(\mathbf{x}_j) < 0$ (i.e. when the instance x_j is not correctly classified). The algorithm is reiterated until it converges to a consistent solution (i.e. $R_{\text{emp}} = [f_\alpha, \mathbf{z}] = 0$).

As for the Primal Perceptron algorithm, it is guaranteed that the Kernel Perceptron algorithm converges in a finite number of steps when it is trained from linearly separable data sets, providing an alternative way to estimate the best separating hyperplane that can be used in all those cases in which feature mappings cannot be performed explicitly. Kernel Perceptron is then an instance-based learning algorithm.

Support Vector Machines in the Dual Space

As for the Kernel Perceptron algorithm, we can define the SVM learning problem in a dual space, in which a kernel function K is adopted to estimate the similarities among the objects instead of defining an explicit feature mapping for them. The vector α can be estimated in the dual space by applying the

---

[5] In Sect. A.5 we illustrate the basic properties of this class of functions.

technique of Lagrange multipliers to the optimization problem defined in A.15, obtaining the following *Wolfe Dual* formulation

$$\text{maximize} \quad \alpha^{\mathrm{T}}\mathbf{1} - \frac{1}{2}\alpha^{\mathrm{T}}\mathbf{y}(\mathbf{G} + Cm\mathbf{I})\mathbf{y}\alpha \tag{A.25}$$

$$\text{subject to} \quad \mathbf{0} \leqslant \alpha \tag{A.26}$$

where $\mathbf{G}$ is the Gram Matrix of K at $\mathbf{x}$ (i.e. $\mathbf{G}_{i,j} = K(x_i, x_j)$ for each $x_i, x_j \in \mathbf{x}$), and α^{T} denote the transpose of α.

In this formulation, all the information required by the algorithm is the Gram Matrix $\mathbf{G}$ and the class assignments $\mathbf{y}$. Explicit feature mappings for the objects in the instance space can then be avoided altogether.

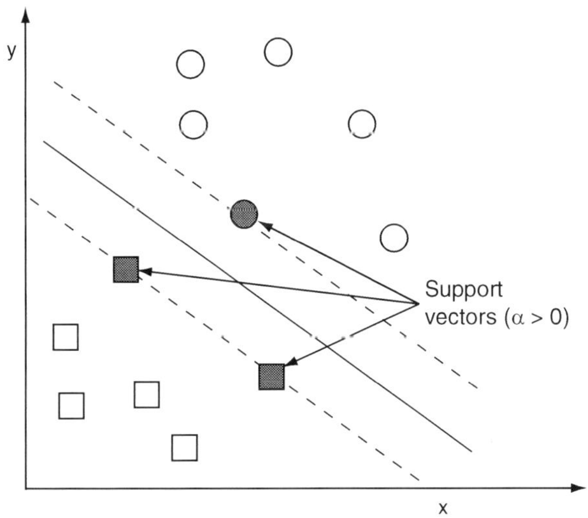

Fig. A.4. Support Vectors

It is possible to show that most of the parameters α_i estimated by the SVM algorithm are 0. All the objects $x_i \in \mathbf{x}$ such that $\alpha_i > 0$ are called Support Vectors. Support Vectors are all those objects that lie closer to the boundary, as illustrated by Fig. A.4. The complexity of the SVM algorithm during classification is then linear on the number of Support Vectors, allowing a very efficient classification. On the other hand, the training phase has higher complexity. In many implementations it is quadratic on the number of training objects, because the Gram Matrix is evaluated before solving the optimization problem.

A.5 Kernel Functions

Kernel functions are similarity functions exploited by linear classifiers to estimate the best separating hyperplane in a dual space. As illustrated in the previous section, the only requirement we ask for a similarity function to be a valid kernel is that it should be equivalent, at least in principle, to a dot product in a feature space.[6] A kernel is then a function $K : \mathcal{X} \times \mathcal{X} \rightarrow \mathbb{R}$ such that

$$K(x_i, x_j) \stackrel{\text{def}}{=} \langle \mathbf{\Phi}(x_i), \mathbf{\Phi}(x_j) \rangle \tag{A.27}$$

where $\mathbf{\Phi} : \mathcal{X} \rightarrow \mathcal{K}$ is a feature mapping.

Of course, not every similarity function is a kernel because, by definition, kernels should be equivalent to some dot product in a feature space. The *Mercer Theorem* provides a viable condition to guarantee that a function is a kernel: $K : \mathcal{X} \times \mathcal{X} \rightarrow \mathbb{R}$ is a kernel if and only if for each $\mathbf{x} \subseteq \mathcal{X}$ such that $|\mathbf{x}| = r$ and $r \in \mathbb{N}$, the Gram Matrix of K at $\mathbf{x}$ is positive semidefinite. This theorem is very important because it opens new perspectives to define kernel functions that only *implicitly* corresponds to a feature mapping $\mathbf{\Phi}$.

Kernel functions can also be composed in a way that the resulting function is still a valid kernel. Then, if $K_1 : \mathcal{X} \times \mathcal{X} \rightarrow \mathbb{R}$ and $K_2 : \mathcal{X} \times \mathcal{X} \rightarrow \mathbb{R}$ are two kernels, the functions $K_c : \mathcal{X} \times \mathcal{X} \rightarrow \mathbb{R}$ defined by the following equations are kernels:

- $K_c(x_i, x_j) = K_1(x_i, x_j) + K_2(x_i, x_j)$
- $K_c(x_i, x_j) = c \cdot K_1(x_i, x_j) \; c \in \mathbb{R}^+$
- $K_c(x_i, x_j) = K_1(x_i, x_j) + c \; , \; c \in \mathbb{R}^+$
- $K_c(x_i, x_j) = K_1(x_i, x_j) \cdot K_2(x_i, x_j)$
- $K_c(x_i, x_j) = f(x_i) \cdot f(x_j) \; , \; \forall f | f : \mathcal{X} \rightarrow \mathbb{R}$
- $K_c(x_i, x_j) = (K_1(x_i, x_j) + c)^\theta \; , \; c \in \mathbb{R}^+$ and $\theta \in \mathbb{N}$ (Polynomial Kernel)
- $K_c(x_i, x_j) = e^{\left(\frac{K_1(x_1, x_2)}{\sigma^2}\right)} \; , \; \sigma \in \mathbb{R}^+$ (Gaussian Kernel)
- $K_c(x_i, x_j) = \frac{K_1(x_1, x_2)}{\sqrt{K_1(x_1, x_1) \times K_1(x_2, x_2)}}$ (cosine)

In summary we can define a kernel function by adopting different strategies: (i) providing an *explicit* feature mapping $\mathbf{\Phi} : \mathcal{X} - \mathbb{R}^n$, (ii) defining a similarity function satisfying the Mercer conditions and (iii) composing different kernels.

A.6 Kernels for Text Processing

Kernel Methods have been successfully exploited to approach a wide variety of NLP tasks, such as Text Categorization [42], Named Entity Recognition

[6] This requirement is necessary to allow the substitution $\langle \mathbf{x}, \mathbf{x_i} \rangle = \langle \mathbf{\Phi}(x), \mathbf{\Phi}(x_i) \rangle = K(x, x_i)$ in Eq. A.23.

[28], Word Sense Disambiguation [29] and Semantic Role Labeling [68]. Kernel Methods can be applied to a particular categorization task when an appropriate kernel function has been specified for the application domain. A wide variety of kernel functions have been proposed in the NLP literature, providing a viable framework to easily develop supervised NLP systems. In fact, the kernel function is the only task dependent component of the learning algorithm. Developing a NLP system in the framework of kernel methods is basically the operation of defining appropriate kernel functions for the linguistic phenomena we are modeling.

Kernel functions can also be composed, by exploiting the properties illustrated in Sect. A.5. It is then possible to take into account different aspects of similarity simultaneously, while modeling them independently. The approach we adopt throughout this book is to define a basic set of kernel functions to deal with the most fundamental linguistic phenomena, and to compose them by exploiting the following combination schema.

$$K_C(x_i, x_j) = \sum_{l=1}^{n} \frac{K_l(x_i, x_j)}{\sqrt{K_l(x_j, x_j) K_l(x_i, x_i)}} \tag{A.28}$$

Some NLP works [29, 68] empirically show the effectiveness of this combination schema, demonstrating that the systems exploiting the combined kernels always improve over the best involved ones.

In our applications, we used the combination schema defined above to combine a set of basic kernels, explicitly developed to model the most fundamental linguistic phenomena. For example, the WSD system presented in [29] is basically implemented by combining two kernels (i.e. a Gap Weighted Subsequence Kernel and a Domain Kernel), to take into account both syntagmatic and paradigmatic relations.

As far as text processing is concerned, the most basic linguistic objects we deal with are texts, sequences and trees. In the following subsections we will describe a set of kernel functions that can be used to estimate the similarity among them.

Kernels for Texts

In general, the similarity among texts is estimated by considering their topics, while other aspects of similitude are less relevant.[7] Topics can be compared by measuring the conceptual overlapping among texts, and other stylistic and rhetorical features can be skipped altogether.

[7] There exist a wide variety of tasks for which it is required to take into account different features, as for example authorship identification [23] and sentiment analysis [72]. In this appendix we will not discuss them.

Vector Space Kernel

After a tokenization step, natural language texts can be described by means of bag-of-words (i.e. unordered sets of terms with associated frequencies in a text). As argued in Sect. 3.2, a bag-of-word representation allows us to compare the topic similarity among texts in the Vector Space Model. The Vector Space Kernel is defined by:

$$K(t_i, t_j) = \langle \mathbf{t_i}, \mathbf{t_j} \rangle = \sum_{z=1}^{k} F(w_z, t_i) \cdot F(w_z, t_j) \tag{A.29}$$

where $F(w, t)$ is the term frequency of w in the text t and $\mathbf{t} = \Phi(t) = (F(w_1, t), F(w_2, t), \ldots, F(w_k, t))$ is the bag-of-words feature mapping for the text t. The complexity of the Vector Space Kernel is linear in the sum of the text lengths (i.e. $O(|t_i| + |t_j|)$).

Some problems are generated by the effect of document length in the similarity estimation. In fact, the vector's norm is proportional to the text's length, overestimating the similarity for longer texts. This effect can be avoided by adopting a cosine metric:

$$K(t_i, t_j) = \left\langle \frac{\mathbf{t}_i}{\|\mathbf{t}_i\|}, \frac{\mathbf{t}_j}{\|\mathbf{t}_j\|} \right\rangle = \frac{K(t_i, t_j)}{\sqrt{K(t_i, t_i) K(t_j, t_j)}} \tag{A.30}$$

Polynomial Kernel

As far as topic similarity is concerned, texts can also be represented by means of tuples of words. In fact, ambiguous words such as virus can be disambiguated by observing that other words co-occur in the same text, as for example computer. The couple `(virus,computer)` is then more informative than the term virus itself, and can be used as a feature for document indexing. If performed explicitly, such an indexing strategy would generate a very huge feature space, (i.e. the embedding space has $|\mathcal{V}|^b$ dimensions, where b is the number of elements for each tuple). The same operation can be modeled more efficiently by applying a Polynomial Kernel (see Sect. A.5) of degree r to the Vector Space Kernel described in the previous paragraph:

$$K(t_i, t_j) = (\langle \mathbf{t}_i, \mathbf{t}_i \rangle + 1)^r \tag{A.31}$$

Evidently, the operation of applying a polynomial kernel does not increase the complexity of the kernel function to which it is applied. Most of the available SVM packages have a default implementation for the Polynomial Kernel.

Semantic Kernels

It is also possible to design "more informed" kernel functions, taking into account information provided by external knowledge sources. This information can be incorporated in the kernel function in several ways. In particular it is possible to take into account additional lexical information by defining a linear mapping from the Vector Space Model, in which texts are originally represented, into a semantic space, indexed by concepts instead of words. The Semantic Kernel provide a viable framework to perform this operation. It is defined by

$$K(t_i, t_j) = \langle \mathbf{t}_i \mathbf{S}, \mathbf{t}_j \mathbf{S} \rangle \tag{A.32}$$

where $\mathbf{S}$ is a $k \times k'$ matrix encoding lexical information, such as term representativeness, term similarity and domain relations. Lexical information can be extracted from different knowledge sources (e.g. lexical databases, unsupervised learning from corpora).

Semantic Kernels can be used to encode a term weighting schema, in order to give higher relevance to the more expressive terms. A very common weighting schema is the Inverse Document Frequency (IDF). In its kernelized version, this operation can be performed by simply substituting $\mathbf{S} = \mathbf{I}^{\mathrm{IDF}}$ in Eq. A.32, where $\mathbf{I}^{\mathrm{IDF}}$ is a diagonal matrix representing the IDF of each term (i.e. $\mathbf{I}^{\mathrm{IDF}}{}_{i,i} = \frac{1}{|\{t \in \mathcal{T} | F(w_i,t)>0\}|}$) . The IDF measure is estimated from an external corpus $\mathcal{T}$ and then used into the supervised learning process.

More elaborated mappings can be defined, for example by exploiting term similarities acquired form large corpora or domain relations. A very basic model to perform this operation is the Generalized VSM [95], obtained by setting $\mathbf{S} = \mathbf{T}\mathbf{T}^{\mathrm{T}}$ (i.e. the term-by-term matrix) in Eq. A.32. The generated mapping is not sparse and takes into account second order similarity relations among terms.

In the literature, many other possibilities have been proposed. For example the matrix $\mathbf{S}$ can be acquired from term clustering on a large corpus (see Sect. 3.5) or it can be defined on the basis of existing manually compiled lexical databases [4].

Kernels for Sequences

As far as NLP applications are concerned, very often we have to deal with sequences: words are sequences of characters, syntagmatic relations are established by sequences of words. Sequences are then analyzed to measure morphological similarity, to detect multiwords and to represent syntagmatic relations. Syntagmatic relations have to be analyzed in a wide variety of NLP tasks, such as Named Entity Recognition [28] and Words Sense Disambiguation [85].

In general, the strategy adopted to model syntagmatic relations is to provide bigrams and trigrams of collocated words as features to describe local contexts, and each word is regarded as a different instance to classify. For instance, occurrences of a given class of named entities (such as *names of persons*) can be discriminated in texts by recognizing word patterns in their local contexts. If for example, the token Rossi is preceded by the token Prof., The former is very likely to be the name of a person. Another example is the Word Sense Disambiguation task, in which it is necessary to analyze syntagmatic relations in the local context of the word to be disambiguated. State-of-the-art Word Sense Disambiguation systems adopt a very rich feature set, composed of bigrams and trigrams in the local context of the word to be disambiguated. Syntagmatic features are very difficult to be modeled, because they typically generate huge feature spaces when extracted explicitly. In addition, token shifting and sparse bigrams are very hard to represent.

As an alternative, kernel functions for sequences can be used. In the literature those kernels have been called String Kernels or Sequence Kernels. The general idea of such kernels is to compare two sequences of symbols by counting the number of subsequences they have in common.

More formally, let Σ be a finite set of symbols (i.e. the *alphabet*), a string $s = s_1, s_2, \ldots, s_{|s|}$ is any finite sequence of symbols $s_i \in \Sigma$, including the *empty sequence* ϵ. Σ^n is the set of all the possible strings of length n and $\Sigma^* = \cup_{n=0}^{\infty} \Sigma^n$ is the set of all the possible strings that can be generated by adopting symbols from Σ. We say that $s = t$ if s and t are identical and we denote by st the string obtained by concatenating the strings s and t. We say that t is a *substring* of s if there are (possibly empty) strings u and v such that $s = utv$. For any i, j such that $1 \leqslant i \leqslant j \leqslant s$, we say that $s(i : j)$ is the substring $s_i, \ldots, s_j$.

Strings are sequences of contiguous symbols. Sometimes we are also interested in detecting subsequences composed by non contiguous elements. We say that the string u is a *subsequence* of s if there exist indices $\mathbf{i} = (i_1, \ldots, i_{|u|})$ such that $1 \leqslant i_1 < \ldots < i_{|u|} \leqslant |s|$ and $u_j = s_{i_j}$, for all $i = 1, \ldots, |u|$. We also denote the subsequence so obtained by the shorthand notation $u = s[\mathbf{i}]$. The number of symbols covered by the subsequence is provided by $l(\mathbf{i}) = i_{|u|} - i_1 + 1$. For example $s =$ structure is a string in the alphabet $\Sigma = \{s, t, r, u, c, e\}$ and $l(s) = 9$. The string $u =$ uct is the substring $s(4 : 6)$ of length 3. The string tcur is the subsequence $s(\mathbf{i})$ characterized by indices $\mathbf{i} = (2, 5, 7, 8)$ and $l(s(\mathbf{i})) = 7$.

Below we will present a set of kernels that can be used to measure the similarity among sequences. All of them can be explicitly defined by embedding maps $\Phi : \Sigma^* \rightarrow \mathcal{F}$ to a vectorial space $\mathcal{F}$, whose dimensions are indexed by a set of strings $\mathbf{s} \subseteq \Sigma^p$ of fixed length p. Kernel functions for sequences differ with respect to the particular feature set they adopt and the feature weighting schema. Below we define the Spectrum Kernel, the Fixed Length Subsequence Kernel and the Gap Weighted Subsequence Kernel.

Spectrum Kernel

The *p-spectrum* of a sequence is the histogram of the frequencies of all its substrings of length p. It generates the following features

$$\Phi_u^p(s) = |\{(v_1, v_2) : s = v_1 u v_2\}|, u \in \Sigma^p \tag{A.33}$$

The p-spectrum kernel is then defined as

$$k_p(s,t) = \langle \Phi^p(s), \Phi^p(t) \rangle = \sum_{u \in \Sigma^p} \Phi^p_u(s) \Phi^p_u(t) \tag{A.34}$$

The Spectrum Kernel returns the number of common (contiguous) substrings of length p. For example, Tab. A.1 illustrate the feature mapping associated to the strings car, cat and cut by the Spectrum Kernel of length 2. The similarity among car and cat is then 1, while the similarity among both car and cut and cat and cut is 0.

Table A.1. Feature mapping generated by the 2-Spectrum Kernel for the strings car, cat and cut

	c-a	a-r	a-t	c-u	u-t
Φ^2(car)	1	1	0	0	0
Φ^2(cat)	1	0	1	0	0
Φ^2(cut)	0	0	0	1	1

The explicit computation of this feature mapping is polynomial in the length of the string (i.e. $O(|s|^p)$).

Fixed Length Subsequence Kernel

The Fixed Length Subsequence Kernel compare two strings by counting the number of all contiguous and non-contiguous subsequences of length p they have in common. It is defined by the following feature mapping

$$\Phi^p_u(s) = |\{\mathbf{i} : u = s(\mathbf{i})\}|, u \in \Sigma^p \tag{A.35}$$

This kernel improves the similarity estimation provided by the Spectrum Kernel because it generates a wider feature space, where both sparse subsequences and substrings are considered. For example, the similarity among cat and cut is now 1, as illustrated by Tab. A.2. In fact, the (new) sparse sequence a-t is associated to both cat and cut, in contrast to the example illustrated in Tab. A.1, where they have similarity 0.

Table A.2. Feature mapping generated by the Fixed Length Subsequence Kernel for the strings car, cat and cut

	c-a	c-r	a-r	c-t	a-t	c-u	u-t
Φ^2(car)	1	1	1	0	0	0	0
Φ^2(cat)	1	0	0	1	1	0	0
Φ^2(cut)	0	0	0	1	0	1	1

The explicit computation of this feature mapping is exponential in the length of the string.

Gap Weighted Subsequence Kernel

The Gap Weighted Subsequence Kernel works in the same feature space as before, but it assigns different weights to subsequences, according to how spread they are in the original strings: the more spread the subsequence, the lower its weight. This intuition is represented by defining the following feature mapping:

$$\Phi_u^p(s) = \sum_{\mathbf{i}:u=s(\mathbf{i})} \lambda^{l(\mathbf{i})}, u \in \Sigma^p \tag{A.36}$$

where $\lambda \in]0,1]$. When $\lambda = 1$ this kernel is equivalent to the Fixed Length Subsequence Kernel, if $\lambda \to 0$ it approximates the p-Spectrum Kernel.

Kernel for Trees

Another basic data structure to be analyzed when dealing with text processing are trees. In fact, sentences in texts can be represented by means of parse trees, describing their syntactic structure. In addition, the structure of XML documents is naturally represented by means of trees.

A tree T is a direct connected acyclic graph in which each vertex (node) except one (i.e. the *root* $r(T)$) has in-degree one. Nodes with out-degree 0 are called *leafs*, the remaining ones are called *internal nodes*. With the symbol $\mathcal{T}$ we denote the set of all the possible trees. A **subtree** is a connected subgraph of a tree. In the definition provided by [12], the tree kernel generates a feature $\phi_S(T)$ for each possible tree $S \in \mathcal{T}$ returning 1 if S is a subtree of T, 0 otherwise. The kernel function is defined in analogy to Eq. A.6.

Convolution Kernels

Evaluating the Tree and the Sequence Kernels by performing the explicit feature mappings described in Sect. A.6 and A.6 is computationally prohibitive. As an alternative, the similarity among structured objects can be evaluated by means of recursive formulations by exploiting dynamic programming techniques. In particular there exists a very important family of kernels, namely *convolution kernels*, that can be used to measure the similarity among generic structured data. Convolution kernels decompose complex structures into finite sets of tuples of subcomponents. There exist efficient implementations of all the string and tree kernels we presented in the preceding sections, based on convolution kernels, that allows us to estimate the similarity among instances by decreasing sensibly the complexity of the problem. A very detailed presentation of all these algorithms is provided by [81].[8]

[8] An efficient implementation of the tree kernel algorithm can be downloaded from `http://ai-nlp.info.uniroma2.it/moschitti/Tree-Kernel.htm`.

References

1. E. Agirre, O. Ansa, D. Martínez, and E. Hovy. Enriching WordNet concepts with topic signatures. In *Proceedings of the SIGLEX Workshop on "WordNet and Other Lexical Resources: Applications, Extensions and Customizations"*, 2001.
2. E. Agirre and G. Rigau. Word sense disambiguation using conceptual density. In *Proceedings of the 16th International Conference on Computational Linguistics (COLING-96)*, pages 16–22, Copenhagen, Denmark, 1996.
3. H. Avancini, A. Lavelli, B. Magnini, F. Sebastiani, and R. Zanoli. Expanding domain-specific lexicons by term categorization. In *Proceedings of the 2003 ACM Symposium on Applied Computing*, pages 793–797, 2003.
4. R. Basili, M. Cammisa, and A. Moschitti. Effective use of WordNet semantics via kernel-based learning. In *Proceedings of the 9th Conference on Computational Natural Language Learning (CoNLL-2005)*, pages 1–8, Ann Arbor, Michigan, June 2005.
5. R. Bekkerman, R. El-Yaniv, N. Tishby, and Y. Winter. Distributional word clusters vs. words for text categorization. *Journal of Machine Learning Research*, 1:1183–1208, 2002.
6. A. Ben-Hur, D. Horn, H.T. Siegelmann, and V. Vapnik. Support vector clustering. *Journal of Machine Learning Research*, 2:125–137, 2001.
7. L. Bentivogli, P. Forner, B. Magnini, and E. Pianta. Revising the WordNet domains hierarchy: semantics, coverage and balancing. In *Proceedings of the COLING-2004 Workshop on Multilingual Linguistic Resources*, pages 364–370, Geneva, Switzerland, August 2004.
8. A. Blum and T. Mitchell. Combining labeled and unlabeled data with co-training. In *COLT: Proceedings of the Workshop on Computational Learning Theory, Morgan Kaufmann Publishers*, 1998.
9. C. J. C. Burges. A tutorial on support vector machines for pattern recognition. *Knowledge Discovery and Data Mining*, 1998.
10. C. Callison-Burch, D. Talbot, and M. Osborne. Statistical machine translation with word- and sentence-aligned parallel corpora. In *Proceedings of the 42nd Annual Meeting of the Association for Computational Linguistics (ACL-2004)*, Barcelona, Spain, 2004.

11. R. L. Cannon, J. V. Dave, and J. C. Bezdek. Efficient implementation of the fuzzy c-means clustering algorithms. *IEEE Transactions on Pattern Analysis and Machine Intelligence*, 8(2):248–255, 1986.
12. M. Collins and N. Duffy. New ranking algorithms for parsing and tagging: Kernels over discrete structures, and the voted perceptron. In *Proceedings of the 40th Annual Meeting of the Association for Computational Linguistics (ACL-02)*, 2002.
13. M. Collins and Y. Singer. Unsupervised models for named entity classification. In *Proceedings of the 4th Conference on Empirical Methods in Natural Language Processing (EMNLP-99)*, College Park, MD, USA, 1999.
14. J. P. Comaroni, J. Beall, W. E. Matthews, and G. R. New, editors. *Dewey Decimal Classification and Relative Index*. Forest Press, Albany, New York, 20th edition, 1989.
15. E. Coseriu. Pour une sémantique diachronique structurale. *Travaux de Linguistique et de Littérature*, 2(1):139–186, 1964.
16. N. Cristianini, J. Shawe-Taylor, and H. Lodhi. Latent semantic kernels. *Journal of Intelligent Information Systems*, 18(2-3):127–152, March-May 2002.
17. I. Dagan. Contextual word similarity. In Rob Dale, Hermann Moisl, and Harold Somers, editors, *Handbook of Natural Language Processing*, chapter 19, pages 459–476. Marcel Dekker Inc, 2000.
18. I. Dagan and A. Itai. Word sense disambiguation using a second language monolingual corpus. *Computational Linguistics*, 20(4):536–596, 1994.
19. I. Dagan, Y. Karov, and D. Roth. Mistake-driven learning in text categorization. In *Proceedings of the 2nd Conference on Empirical Methods in Natural Language Processing (EMNLP-97)*, 1997.
20. F. de Saussure. *Cours de linguistique générale*. Payot, Paris, 1922.
21. B. Decadt, V. Hoste, W. Daelemens, and A. van den Bosh. GAMBL, genetic algorithm optimization of memory-based WSD. In *Proceedings of SENSEVAL-3: Third International Workshop on the Evaluation of Systems for the Semantic Analysis of Text*, Barcelona, Spain, July 2004.
22. S. Deerwester, S. Dumais, G. Furnas, T. Landauer, and R. Harshman. Indexing by latent semantic analysis. *Journal of the American Society of Information Science*, 1990.
23. M. Diab, J. Schuster, and P. Bock. A preliminary statistical investigation into the impact of an n-gram analysis approach based on word syntactic categories toward text author classification. In *Proceedings of the 6th International Conference on Artificial Intelligence Applications*, 1998.
24. G. Escudero, L. Marquez, and G. Rigau. An empirical study of the domain dependence of supervised word sense disambiguation systems. In *Proceedings of the 5th Conference on Empirical Methods in Natural Language Processing (EMNLP-2000)*, pages 172–180, Hong Kong, 2000.
25. C. Fellbaum. *WordNet. An Electronic Lexical Database.* MIT Press, 1998.
26. W. Gale, K. Church, and D. Yarowsky. One sense per discourse. In *Proceedings of the ARPA Workshop on Speech and Natural Language Processing*, 1992.
27. E. Gaussier, J. M. Renders, I. Matveeva, C. Goutte, and H. Dejean. A geometric view on bilingual lexicon extraction from comparable corpora. In *Proceedings of the 42nd Annual Meeting of the Association for Computational Linguistics (ACL-04)*, Barcelona, Spain, July 2004.

28. A. Gliozzo, C. Giuliano, and R. Rinaldi. Instance filtering for entity recognition. *ACM SIGKDD Explorations, Special Issue on Natural Language Processing and Text Mining*, 7(1):11–18, June 2005.
29. A. Gliozzo, C. Giuliano, and C. Strapparava. Domain kernels for word sense disambiguation. In *Proceedings of the 43rd Annual Meeting of the Association for Computational Linguistics (ACL-05)*, pages 403–410, Ann Arbor, Michigan, June 2005.
30. A. Gliozzo, B. Magnini, and C. Strapparava. Unsupervised domain relevance estimation for word sense disambiguation. In *Proceedings of the 2004 Conference on Empirical Methods in Natural Language Processing (EMNLP-04)*, Barcelona, Spain, July 2004
31. A. Gliozzo and C. Strapparava. Domain kernels for text categorization. In *Proceedings of the 9th Conference on Computational Natural Language Learning (CoNLL-2005)*, pages 56–63, 2005.
32. A. Gliozzo, C. Strapparava, and I. Dagan. Unsupervised and supervised exploitation of semantic domains in lexical disambiguation. *Computer Speech and Language*, 18(3):275–299, 2004.
33. A. Gliozzo, C. Strapparava, and I. Dagan. Investigating unsupervised learning for text categorization bootstrapping. In *Proceedings of the Conference on Empirical Methods in Natural Language Processing (EMNLP-2005)*, 2005.
34. J. Gonzalo, F. Verdejio, I. Chugur, and J. Cigarran. Indexing with WordNet synsets can improve text retrieval. In *Proceedings of the ACL Workshop on the Usage of WordNet in Natural Language Processing Systems*, pages 38–44, Montreal, Quebec, Canada, August 1998.
35. J. Guthrie, L. Guthrie, Y. Wilks, and H. Aidinejad. Subject-dependent cooccurence and word sense disambiguation. In *Proceedings of the 29th Annual Meeting of the ACL*, pages 146–152, Berkeley, California, June 1991.
36. J. Hammerton, M. Osborne, S. Armstrong, and W. Daelemans. Introduction to Special Issue on Machine Learning Approaches to Shallow Parsing. *Journal of Machine Learning Research*, 2(3):551–558, March 2002.
37. F. Höppner, F. Klawonn, R. Kruse, and T. Runkler. *Fuzzy Cluster Analysis*. Wiley, 1999.
38. M. Hearst and H. Schütze. Customizing a lexicon to better suit a computational task. In *Proceedings of the ACL SIGLEX Workshop on Acquisition of Lexical Knowledge from Text*, 1993.
39. R. Herbrich. *Learning Kernel Classifiers: Theory and Algorithms*. MIT Press, 2002.
40. T. Joachims. Making large-scale SVM learning practical. In B. Schölkopf, C. Burges, and A. Smola, editors, *Advances in kernel methods: support vector learning*, chapter 11, pages 169–184. MIT Press, 1999.
41. T. Joachims. Transductive inference for text classification using support vector machines. In *Proceedings of the Sixteenth International Conference on Machine Learning (ICML 99)*, pages 200–209, Bled, Slovenia, June 1999
42. T. Joachims. *Learning to Classify Text using Support Vector Machines*. Kluwer Academic Publishers, 2002.
43. M.J. Kearns and U.V. Vazirani. *An Introduction to Computational Learning Theory*. MIT Press, 1994.
44. A. Kilgarriff. Gold standard datasets for evaluating word sense disambiguation programs. *Computer Speech and Language*, 12(4):453–472, 1998. Special Issue on Evaluation of Speech and Language Technology.

45. A. Kilgarriff and M. Palmer. Introduction to the special issue on SENSEVAL. *Computers and the Humanities*, 34(1-2):1–13, 2000.
46. Y. Ko and J. Seo. Automatic text categorization by unsupervised learning. In *Proceedings of the 18th International Conference on Computational Linguistics (COLING-2000)*, 2000.
47. Y. Ko and J. Seo. Learning with unlabeled data for text categorization using bootstrapping and feature projection techniques. In *Proceedings of the 42nd Annual Meeting of the Association for Computational Linguistics (ACL-04)*, Barcelona, Spain, July 2004.
48. P. Koehn and K. Knight. Learning a translation lexicon from monolingual corpora. In *Proceedings of the ACL-02 Workshop on Unsupervised Lexical Acquisition*, Philadelphia, July 2002.
49. R. Krovetz. More than one sense per discourse. Technical report, NEC Research Institute, Princeton, 1998.
50. T. K. Landauer and S. T. Dumais. A solution to Plato's problem: The latent semantic analysis theory of the acquisition, induction, and representation of knowledge. *Psychological Review*, 1997.
51. S. Landes, C. Leacock, and R. I. Tengi. Building semantic concordances. In C. Fellbaum, editor, *WordNet: An Electronic Lexical Database.* MIT Press, 1998.
52. M. Lesk. Automated sense disambiguation using machine-readable dictionaries:how to tell a pine cone from an ice cream cone. In *Proceedings of the 1986 SIGDOC Conference*, pages 24–26, Toronto, Canada, June 1986.
53. M. Littman, S. Dumais, and T. Landauer. Automatic cross-language information retrieval using latent semantic indexing. In G. Grefenstette, editor, *Cross Language Information Retrieval*, pages 51–62. Kluwer Academic Publishers, 1998.
54. B. Liu, X. Li, W. S. Lee, and P. S. Yu. Text classification by labeling words. In *Proceedings of the Nineteenth National Conference on Artificial Intelligence (AAAI-2004)*, San Jose, July 2004.
55. J. Lyons. *Semantics.* Cambridge University Press, 1977.
56. B. Magnini and G. Cavaglià. Integrating subject field codes into WordNet. In *Proceedings of LREC-2000, Second International Conference on Language Resources and Evaluation*, pages 1413–1418, Athens, Greece, June 2000.
57. B. Magnini and C. Strapparava. Improving user modelling with content-based techniques. In *Proceedings of 8th International Conference on User Modeling (UM-2001)*, Sonthofen, Germany, July 2001.
58. B. Magnini, C. Strapparava, G. Pezzulo, and A. Gliozzo. Using domain information for word sense disambiguation. In *Proceedings of SENSEVAL-2: Second International Workshop on Evaluating Word Sense Disambiguation System*, pages 111–114, Toulouse, France, July 2001.
59. B. Magnini, C. Strapparava, G. Pezzulo, and A. Gliozzo. The role of domain information in word sense disambiguation. *Natural Language Engineering*, 8(4):359–373, 2002.
60. L. M. Manevitz and M. Yousef. One-class SVMs for document classification. *Journal of Machine Learning Research*, 2:139–154, 2001.
61. A. McCallum and K. Nigam. Text classification by bootstrapping with keywords, EM and shrinkage. In *Proceedings of the ACL-99 Workshop for Unsupervised Learning in Natural Language Processing*, University of Maryland, June 1999.

62. D. McCarthy, R. Koeling, J. Weeds, and J. Carroll. Finding predominant senses in untagged text. In *Proceedings of the 42nd Annual Meeting of the Association for Computational Linguistics*, pages 280–287, Barcelona, Spain, 2004.
63. D. Melamed. *Empirical Methods for Exploiting Parallel Texts.* MIT Press, 2001.
64. R. Mihalcea and P. Edmonds, editors. *Proceedings of SENSEVAL-3: Third International Workshop on the Evaluation of Systems for the Semantic Analysis of Text*, Barcelona, Spain, July 2004.
65. R. Mihalcea and E. Faruque. Senselearner: Minimally supervised WSD for all words in open text. In *Proceedings of SENSEVAL-3: Third International Workshop on the Evaluation of Systems for the Semantic Analysis of Text*, Barcelona, Spain, July 2004.
66. G. Miller. An on-line lexical database. *International Journal of Lexicography*, 13(4):235–312, 1990.
67. A. Moschitti. *Natural Language Processing and Text Categorization: a study on the reciprocal beneficial interactions.* PhD thesis, University of Rome Tor Vergata, Rome, Italy, May 2003.
68. A. Moschitti. A study on convolution kernel for shallow semantic parsing. In *Proceedings of the 42nd Annual Meeting of the Association for Computational Linguistics (ACL-2004)*, 2004.
69. H. T. Ng. Getting serious about word sense disambiguation. In *Proceedings of the ACL SIGLEX Workshop on Tagging Text with Lexical Semantics: Why, What, and How?*, pages 1–7, Washington, DC, USA, 1996.
70. K. Nigam, A. K. McCallum, S. Thrun, and T. M. Mitchell. Text classification from labeled and unlabeled documents using EM. *Machine Learning*, 39(2/3):103–134, 2000.
71. M. Palmer, C. Fellbaum, S. Cotton, L. Delfs, and H.T. Dang. English tasks: All-words and verb lexical sample. In *Proceedings of SENSEVAL-2*, Toulouse, France, July 2001.
72. B. Pang and L. Lee. A sentimental education: sentiment analysis using subjectivity summarization based on minimum cuts. In *Proceedings of the 42nd Annual Meeting of the Association for Computational Linguistics (ACL-2004)*, pages 271–278, 2004.
73. D. Pérez, A. Gliozzo, C. Strapparava, E. Alfonseca, P. Rodríguez, and B. Magnini. Automatic assessment of students' free-text answers underpinned by the combination of a BLEU-inspired algorithm and latent semantic analysis. In *Proceedings of FLAIRS-2005*, Clearwater Beach, Florida, May 16-18 2005.
74. W. Porzig. Wesenhafte Bedeutungsbeziehungen. *Beiträge zur Geschichte der deutschen Sprache und Literatur*, 58, 1934.
75. J. Preiss and D. Yarowsky, editors. *Proceedings of SENSEVAL-2: Second International Workshop on Evaluating Word Sense Disambiguation Systems*, Toulouse, France, 2002.
76. P. Proctor. *Longman Dictionary of Contemporary English.* 1978.
77. P. Resnik and D. Yarowsky. A perspective on word sense disambiguation methods and their evaluation. In *Proceedings of the ACL SIGLEX Workshop on Tagging Text with Lexical Semantics: Why, What and How?*, pages 79–86, Washington, DC, USA, 1997.

78. G. Salton and M.H. McGill. *Introduction to Modern Information Retrieval.* McGraw-Hill, New York, 1983.
79. H. Schutze and J. Pedersen. Information retrieval based on word senses. In *Symposium on Document Analysis and Information Retrieval*, 1995.
80. F. Sebastiani. Machine learning in automated text categorization. *ACM Computing Surveys*, 34(1):1–47, 2002.
81. J. Shawe-Taylor and N. Cristianini. *Kernel Methods for Pattern Analysis.* Cambridge University Press, 2004.
82. B. W. Silverman. *Density Estimation for Statistics and Data Analysis.* Chapman and Hall, 1986.
83. S. Small. *Word Expert Parsing: A Theory of Distributed Word-Based Natural Language Understanding.* Ph.D. Thesis, Department of Computer Science, University of Maryland, 1980.
84. M. Stevenson and Y. Wilks. Combining weak knowledge sources for sense disambiguation. In *Proceedings of the International Joint Conference in Artificial Intelligence (IJCAI-99)*, pages 884–889, Stockholm, Sweden, 1999.
85. C. Strapparava, C. Giuliano, and A. Gliozzo. Pattern abstraction and term similarity for word sense disambiguation: IRST at Senseval-3. In *Proceedings of SENSEVAL-3: Third International Workshop on the Evaluation of Systems for the Semantic Analysis of Text*, Barcelona, Spain, July 2004.
86. N. Tishby, F. Pereira, and W. Bialek. The information bottleneck method. In *Proceedings of the 37th Annual Allerton Conference on Communication, Control and Computing*, pages 368–377, 1999.
87. J. Trier. *Der deutsche Wortschatz im Sinnbezirk des Verstandes.* Heidelberg, 1931.
88. J. Trier. Das sprachliche Feld. Eine Auseinandersetzung. *Neue Fachrbücher für Wissenschaft und Jugendbildung*, 10:428–449, 1934.
89. S. Ullmann. *The Principles of Semantics.* Blackwell, Oxford, 1957.
90. V. Vapnik. *The Nature of Statistical Learning Theory.* Springer, 1995.
91. V. Vapnik, S.E. Golowich, and A. Smola. Support vector method for function approximation, regression estimation, and signal processing. In M. Mozer, M. Jordan, and T. Petsche, editors, *Advances in Neural Information Processing Systems*, pages 281–287. MIT Press, 1997.
92. L.M. Vassilyev. The theory of semantic fields: a survey. *Linguistics*, 137:79–93, 1974.
93. L. Weisgerber. Vom inhaltlichen Aufbau des deutschen Wortschatzes. *Wortfeldforschung*, pages 193–225, 1939.
94. L. Wittgenstein. *Philosophical Investigations.* The Macmillan Company, New York, 1965.
95. S.K.M. Wong, W. Ziarko, and P.C.N. Wong. Generalized vector space model in information retrieval. In *Proceedings of the 8th Annual International ACM SIGIR Conference on Research and Development in Information Retrieval*, 1985.
96. D. Yarowsky. Word-sense disambiguation using statistical models of Roget's categories trained on large corpora. In *Proceedings of the 14th International Conference on Computational Linguistics (COLING-92)*, pages 454–460, Nantes, France, 1992.
97. D. Yarowsky. Unsupervised word sense disambiguation rivaling supervised methods. In *Proceedings of the 33rd Annual Meeting of the Association for Computational Linguistics (ACL-95)*, pages 189–196, Cambridge, MA, 1995.

98. D. Yarowsky and R. Florian. Evaluating sense disambiguation across diverse parameter space. *Natural Language Engineering*, 8(4):293–310, 2002.
99. S. Zelikovitz and H. Hirsh. Using LSI for text classification in the presence of background text. In *Proceedings of the 10th International Conference on Information and Knowledge Management (CIKM'01)*, pages 113–118, Atlanta, USA, 2001.
100. G.K. Zipf. *Human Behavior and the Principle of Least Effort*. Addison-Wesley, 1949.